# Sony vs. Samsung

The Inside Story of the Electronics
Giants' Battle for Global Supremacy

# Sony vs. Samsung

The Inside Story of the Electronics
Giants' Battle for Global Supremacy

Sea-Jin Chang

**WILEY**

John Wiley & Sons (Asia) Pte. Ltd.

This publication is designed to provide accurate and authoritative information with regard to the subject matter covered. It is sold with the understanding that the Publisher is not engaged in rendering professional services. If professional advice or other expert assistance is required, the services of a competent professional person should be sought.

**Other Wiley Editorial Offices**

John Wiley & Sons, Inc., 111 River Street, Hoboken, NJ 07030, USA
John Wiley & Sons Ltd., The Atrium, Southern Gate,
    Chichester PO19 BSQ, England
John Wiley & Sons (Canada) Ltd., 5353 Dundas Street West, Suite 400, Toronto,
    Ontario M9B 6H8, Canada
John Wiley & Sons Australia Ltd., 42 McDougall Street, Milton, Queensland 4064,
    Australia
Wiley-VCH, Boschstrasse 12, D-69469 Weinheim, Germany

**Library of Congress Cataloging-in-Publication Data:**

ISBN 978-0-470-82371-2

Typeset in 11-14 point, Minion Pro by Superskill Graphics Pte. Ltd.
Printed in Singapore by Saik Wah Press Pte. Ltd.
10 9 8 7 6 5 4 3 2 1

# Contents

# Preface

This book emerged out of my own curiosity to understand why Sony's performance, which had dominated the electronics industry for many decades, had dropped so rapidly, while Samsung Electronics, an obscure OEM (Original Equipment Manufacturer) not so many years ago, had emerged from nowhere. I must confess that I was one of the admirers of Sony for its innovative products as well as for its global management. I was fascinated by the late Akio Morita's book, *Made in Japan*, and was impressed by his global mindset and business acumen. This had led me to a research project in 1994–1995 to examine the evolution of Sony's U.S. operation. I had opportunities to meet with many outstanding managers and engineers at Sony including Kunitake Ando, who then was a head of its U.S. operation.

Sony was a role model for many Korean companies, including Samsung Electronics, with which I have maintained a close contact through various projects, and a direct comparison between these two would have been inappropriate at that time. Ten years later, however, the fortunes of these two companies changed dramatically. Sony's performance deteriorated, and Chairman Idei and President Ando had to resign in 2005. On the other hand, Jong-yong Yun, CEO, was applauded for turning Samsung Electronics into one of the most profitable companies in the electronics industry. I felt compelled to find out what had caused their changing fortunes.

Faced with the rapid digitalization of the electronics industry, Sony and Samsung Electronics had pursued rather different strategies. Sony tried to create synergies between hardware and contents by using the network. Samsung Electronics, on the other hand, focused on its parts business, and attempted to secure competitive advantages in end products by being a superior manufacturer. As I dug deeper in the analysis, I became more convinced that the performance differences between Sony and Samsung Electronics could not be attributed to their strategies. Rather, organizational processes and executives' leadership may have made the difference. Sony's independent business units quickly became silos when its top management leadership was questioned. Internal politics among executives further exacerbated its stagnation. On the other hand, the fit between Samsung's strategy in responding to commoditization with speed and its militaristic organization may have contributed to its stellar performance. I further examine the challenges that Samsung Electronics faces, despite its remarkable performance, and evaluate Sony's potential, despite its current struggles.

My endeavor to analyze key strategic decisions by Sony and Samsung Electronics during the last decade would not have been successful without the assistance of Myoung-woo Lee, a 20-year veteran of Samsung Electronics, and, more recently, the president and chairman of Sony Korea. With his unique vantage point of both companies, he not only shared his own perspectives, but also introduced me to executives and managers of both companies for further interviews. I was fortunate enough to have personal interviews with high-level executives (including retirees) of both companies, which would not have been possible without Mr. Lee's introductions. In addition, I had interviews with security analysts and executives of other firms in the electronics industry to get more objective, external opinions. I would like to take this opportunity to thank him for his contributions and assistance.

I am also deeply indebted to several other individuals and organizations. I would like to thank Korea University for providing a special research fund for this project to cover my frequent trips to Japan. I also benefited from discussions with my colleagues at Hitotsubashi University, where I spent the summer of 2007 while preparing the manuscript. John Lafkas, Kyung-hwan Yun, Sejung Seo, Sang-hee Lee,

Young-jae Koh, and Jung-wook Shim provided very helpful editorial and research assistance for the project. I would like to thank Nick Wallwork, my editor at Wiley, and his fellow staff members including Joel Balbin, Fiona Wong, and Pauline Pek, as well as copyeditor Jay Boggis, who all did a wonderful job of turning the manuscript into a book. Last but not least, I would like to thank the executives and managers at Sony and Samsung Electronics who were willing to share their valuable time to meet with me. I cannot name them all here partly because there are too many and partly because most wanted to remain anonymous. I believe in management education. I believe managers can learn from the experience of other firms so that they will not repeat the same mistakes and they can make better informed decisions. Executives and managers from both companies I interviewed were eager to share their own perspectives. I would like to dedicate this book to them.

Sea-Jin Chang

Philadephia
February 2008

# 1

# Sony and Samsung: Portraits of Two Global Competitors

Digital technology... [presents] ... the greatest opportunity for those manufacturers who did not have a top market share in the analog world. If they make the correct changes in strategy, they possibly could leap-frog well-entrenched industry leaders.

*—Steve F. Smith, Editor-in-Chief, TWICE Magazine*

Sony ruled a slower age when it could bring out a new gadget like the Walkman as a luxury item, then gradually lower the price and widen the market over time. Now, since the rise of cheap Asian manufacturing in the 1980s, companies need to bring out a stream of new products that sell immediately at high volume for a relatively low price, and are quickly displaced by the next new thing. Samsung is king of this age.

*—Newsweek*[1]

## The Fall of Sony and the Rise of Samsung Electronics

### A Turning Point
A few years ago, the electronics industry reached a milestone. Sony had long been acknowledged as the world's best electronics manufacturer, but in 2002, Sony's market capitalization fell below Samsung's, which

*Figure 1.1*    The Market Capitalization of Sony and Samsung Electronics

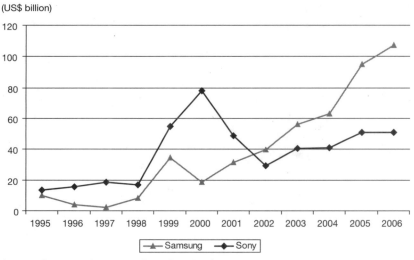

(US$ billion)

*Source:*  Samsung Securities, Sony Fact Book.

had been an obscure memory chip producer not many years ago. Figure 1.1 shows some of the raw data behind this story. By December 2006, Samsung's market capitalization was $106 billion, an increase of 400% since 2000 and twice that of Sony's. Since becoming CEO in 1997, Jong-yong Yun, has become famous for turning Samsung Electronics into one of the most profitable companies in the electronics industry. By contrast, Sony's Chairman Nobuyuki Idei and President Kunitake Ando resigned in 2005 and were succeeded by Howard Stringer and Ryoji Chubachi, respectively.

Sony began from a position of strength. The late Chairman Akio Morita had shown the world that Sony had become a global company. Michael Porter, a strategy guru, praised Sony highly as one of the few Japanese companies that actually had a strategy.[2]

Sony's troubles began, however, after it acquired Columbia Pictures in 1989 (see Figure 1.2). Things turned out so bad that by 1994 it had to write off accumulated losses of $3.5 billion. Sony then restructured its entertainment business to control costs. Sony's profitability peaked in 1997 when it introduced PlayStation, but started to decline again soon afterward, and sales became stagnant. By contrast, although Samsung Electronics' sales and profitability were highly volatile during the late 1990s, its revenue almost doubled between 2000 and 2006, and it had

*Figure 1.2*   Sony and Samsung Electronics' Sales and Profitability (1991–2006)

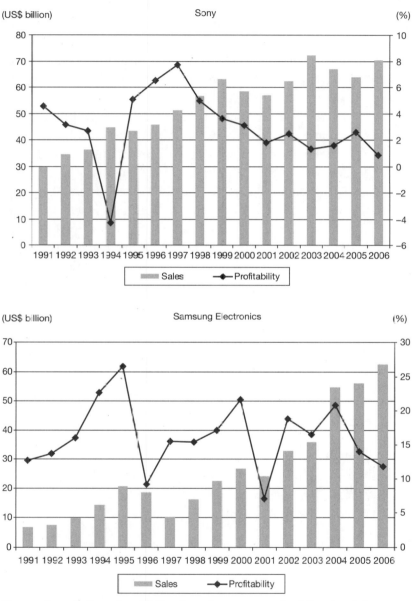

*Source:* Annual Reports and Earnings Announcement of Sony and Samsung, respectively.

Note: Profitability is defined as operating income divided by sales.

a considerably higher rate of profitability than Sony enjoyed during this period.

Some of the best evidence of Samsung's rise and Sony's fall appeared in the changing tones of Sony's top management whenever they spoke about Samsung. Nobuyuki Idei noted in 2002 that "Samsung found Sony a model or a benchmark for their brand image. The product design and the product planning—they have learned from us. So Sony is a very good target for them." To him, Samsung was merely one of the suppliers rather than a potential threat. He continued, "We still believe that Samsung is basically a component company."[3] Just a year later, Kunitake Ando, president of Sony, mentioned that he asked "for a report on what Samsung is doing every week."[4] In 2006, Sony's newly appointed CEO, Howard Stringer, said that "Samsung is a first-rate company and they have a wealth of revenue coming from other areas. But, I think in the high-definition world, which is clearly our strategy for this year, we still have an advantage." Sony was now openly acknowledging that Samsung Electronics had now become its competitor.[5] Some of the popular press even inflicted the ultimate insult on Sony by commenting that it needed a lesson from Samsung. "As he looks for inspiration, Stringer might consider taking a page from Samsung Electronics. The Korean company has taken many of the steps that analysts believe Sony needs to take, ranging from collaborating more with partners to doing a better job taking its cues from the market. In doing so, it has become one of the nimblest players in the business."[6]

**The Media Hype**

Sony had once dominated the electronics industry. So why did its fortunes drop so rapidly, just as Samsung was emerging from out of nowhere? The media have speculated about why the fortunes of these two companies changed so rapidly, but their evaluations are usually superficial and focus only on short-term performance. Often, journalists anoint a CEO as a Best Manager one year, only to dub him the Worst Manager just a few years later.

Sony had been nominated as one of the "World's Most Admired Companies" by *Fortune* in 1997, which commented that "Sony was voted the most effective Asian company at doing business globally, the best company in Asia at wooing and winning topnotch people, and the

*Figure 1.3*   Media's Evaluation of Nobuyuki Idei

Cover image courtesy of *BusinessWeek*.          Photograph by Shonna Valeska

*BusinessWeek*'s TOP 25 Managers of the Year (1999)

Cover image courtesy of *BusinessWeek*.          Photograph by Associated Press

*BusinessWeek*'s Worst Managers of the Year (2004)

most innovative electronics company in the world. Since he took over two years ago, Idei has shaken the place to its foundations, revamping the board of directors, restructuring major divisions, and clamping down on U.S. operations—especially Sony Pictures Entertainment."[7] The magazine's evaluation of Sony and Idei soured, however, soon after the firm's performance deteriorated. *BusinessWeek* had nominated Idei as one of the World's Best Managers in 1997 and 1999. But in 2004, the magazine put him on the World's Worst list when he triggered the so-called Sony shock by announcing that the company had suffered a quarterly loss of about $1 billion, which triggered a sell-off of shares, plunging its stock price nearly 25% in two days.

The most amazing accusation, according to the same magazine, was "Idei's later admission that he himself had been caught off guard by the dismal earnings."[8] He was also criticized for failing to move far enough or fast enough in a corporate restructuring program he had announced in 1999 and for not being able to come up with innovative products. "Sony has pushed great-looking products made from the same digital components that everyone has. So it's no surprise that its CD (Compact Disc) players, digital cameras, and other gadgets become commodities almost as soon as they hit the market."[9] While Stringer and Chubachi, the new management team, stopped the hemorrhage by closing down factories and laying off workers, it is not clear whether Sony can regain its reputation as the world's most innovative consumer electronics powerhouse.

The media often misread up-and-coming firms. A few years ago, everyone wrote about Samsung Electronics as just one of the many anonymous Asian Original Equipment Manufacturing (OEM) companies that dumped cheap, low-quality products in discount stores. Until recently, it was hard to find an article that was favorable of Samsung Electronics. In an article about the Samsung Group that was written right after the financial crisis in 1998, *BusinessWeek* described Samsung Electronics as a company that manufactured commodity chips, such as DRAMs (Dynamic Random Access Memory), and had been badly hurt by the Asian crisis and the downturn of the global chip business. "Senior managers have taken a 10% pay cut. Workers can no longer count on such perks as preschool tuition. At headquarters, the thermostat is now set so low that execs wear thermal underwear."[10]

But fortunes soon changed. In 1997, *Fortune* had named Idei as "Asia's Businessman of the Year." But in 1999 it gave the same title to

Jong-yong Yun of Samsung Electronics. He was now the man who "used Asia's current chaos to reinvent a company that seemed near death."[11] He was also praised for turning "a manufacturer of cheap black-and-white TVs into a $72 billion behemoth that earns more and has a more valuable global brand than archrival Sony."[12]

Popular books such as Thomas Peters and Robert Waterman's *In Search of Excellence*, Jim Collins's *Good to Great*, and Jim Collins and Jerry Porras's *Built to Last* describe the properties of successful companies as success factors that other firms should emulate.[13] But Philip Rosenzweig, author of the *Halo Effect*, argues that those books merely summarize the characteristics of successful firms; they do not identify true success factors. Managers around the world are constantly looking for magic formulas to improve their bottom line. They find it difficult to resist the temptation to emulate firms like acquisition-savvy Cisco or HP, which does such a good job of cultivating employees. Boards are also looking for a charismatic leader such as Steve Jobs in the hope that he or she will bring tremendous instant success with a product like the iPod. Simply copying a corporate culture, leadership, value system, or strategy does not necessarily lead to success, however; these properties are not themselves the success factors.

Rosenzweig calls the tendency to observe the results first and then rationalize the company's strategies the Halo Effect.[14] The real challenge is to compare Samsung Electronics' and Sony's business structures, technology, brands, organizations, and management systems and to explain why these two giants have met with such drastically different fates during the past 10 years.

## Comparison of Sony and Samsung Electronics: Motivations and Limitations

Any comparison of Sony and Samsung Electronics will inevitably be inexact. Sony is a significantly older firm. It was born as a start-up company, while Samsung Electronics began as a subsidiary of Samsung Group and shares that group's company culture and management system. Further, the missions of these firms were very different. Sony was founded in the early years of post-war Japan and has attempted to make consumers' lives more convenient by developing and producing innovative products such as the Walkman and the Compact Disc. Samsung Electronics, by contrast, was founded during Korea's period of rapid industrialization. It created a long-standing identity as a manufacturer of key parts that are essential to the electronics industry. It lived by slogans like "semiconductors are the bread of the electronics business," and "contribute to the nation by industry." Moreover, the cultural differences between Japan and Korea add to the distinctions between these two companies.

In addition, Sony and Samsung Electronics' key businesses are very different. Sony has devoted significant resources not only to the electronics business but also to music, movies, and software. It also has a B2C (business to customer) business structure, and thus sells mainly to end users. In contrast, although the Samsung Group as a whole is extremely diversified, Samsung Electronics produces and sells parts to other electronics firms, and its product portfolio is centered on the electronics industry. Even its mobile phone business is closer to a B2B (business to business) model than it is to B2C. Samsung Electronics sells its products mainly to a small number of operators.

But despite these important differences, a comparison uncovers valuable insights. First, Sony and Samsung Electronics simultaneously compete and cooperate with each other. They compete in the realms of TVs, DVDs, audio, camcorders, digital cameras, and mobile phones. But they cooperate in the production of LCDs (Liquid Crystal Display) through their S-LCD joint venture. Samsung's leading LCD technology and Sony's expertise in product development help both companies gain competitive advantages against their rivals. Further, Samsung Electronics supplies DRAMs and flash memory to Sony, but it purchases CCDs (Charge Couple Device) and batteries from Sony. Comparing two companies that simultaneously compete and cooperate reveals the overall dynamics of how firms in the electronics industry have responded to common trends.

Second, comparing Sony and Samsung Electronics may shed light on how the performance of different firms may change as they try to adjust to rapid technological developments in the electronics industry and how companies should effectively respond to such changes. Firms like Apple and Hewlett-Packard show how volatile the electronics industry can be. For example, Apple had a near-death experience when its Macintosh lines were marginalized by Windows-based personal computers, only to be resurrected by its unexpected success with iPod. Samsung Electronics and Sony have responded somewhat differently to the rapid digitalization of the electronics industry during the past decade. Sony invested in network technology and attempted to create synergy between hardware and software such as music and film. Samsung Electronics focused on manufacturing core parts. Its CEO Yun has a motto: "Stay at the forefront of core technologies and master the manufacturing and you control your future."[15] Sony and Samsung Electronics adopted different strategies as they responded to digitalization. Both strategies have their benefits and shortcomings.

Samsung Electronics and Sony are representative Asian companies, which lead the Korean and Japanese electronics industries. A comparison will reveal important strengths and weaknesses of Asia-based companies. In many cases, these companies are still owned and managed by their founders or founders' families. In many cases the transition to professional managers that is typical in Western firms has not yet occurred. Comparing Samsung Electronics and Sony provides a good perspective on the problems that Asian firms encounter during such transitions.

Finally, both these firms have global ambitions. Because Sony began much earlier than Samsung Electronics and is currently far more globalized, its problems may provide useful lessons to Samsung Electronics, as well as to other Asian companies.

## The History and Business Areas of Sony and Samsung Electronics

### Sony

*The King of AV*
In 1946, the year after Japan's defeat in World War II, Sony was incorporated as the Tokyo Telecommunication Engineering Corporation. Ibuka Masaru, a talented inventor who had developed various electronic devices during the war, brought in Akio Morita as the manager. Masaru and Morita rented a floor of a department store in *Nihonbashi* Tokyo to use as the office and factory, and launched their business with an investment of 190,000 yen and 20 employees. Sony was just one more start-up company in post-war Japan. These founding conditions indelibly marked Sony's development and growth.

Tokyo Telecommunication Engineering Corporation produced vacuum tube voltmeters and communication devices. It even manufactured electric rice cookers and electric floorboards. Sony would manufacture almost anything in order to survive. In 1950, it developed a tape recorder, which it supplied to schools and governments. In 1955, it purchased patent rights for a U.S.-developed transistor and began to produce and sell small transistor radios. In 1955, Morita sold the first transistor radio with the Sony brand in the U.S.

As Sony-brand transistors became a huge hit overseas, the company changed its name to Sony in 1958. Sony is a combination of the Latin word *sonus*, which means sound, and *sonny*, a nickname for a small boy. This name reflected the company's ambition to grow and corresponded to an image of vibrant youth. Sony issued ADRs (American Depository Receipt) on the New York Stock Exchange in 1961, laying a stepping stone toward its development into a global company.

In the 1960s, Sony developed Trinitron technology, which radically upgraded the quality of color TV displays. Its CRT (Cathode Ray Tube) TV, based on Trinitron technology, was immensely popular. Sony's biggest success, however, was the Walkman, a compact cassette tape player that Sony introduced in 1979. It subsequently produced high-quality computer monitors, home VTRs (Video Tape Recorders), CCDs, passport-size camcorders, digital cameras, 3.5 inch floppy disks, CDs, MiniDiscs, and DVDs (Digital Video Disc). In the late 1990s, Sony released WEGA, which applies digital technology to a flat-screen CRT TV. This made it the dominant player in the high-quality TV market.

In 2005, Sony was tied with Philips and Samsung for second in the LCD TV sector. It was first in the digital camcorder sector

*Figure 1.4*    Sony and Samsung's Market Shares in Major Products

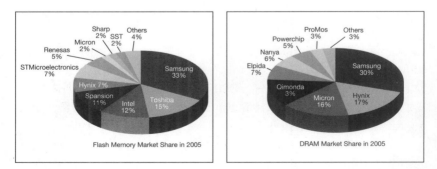

*Figure 1.4* Sony and Samsung's Market Shares in Major Products (cont'd)

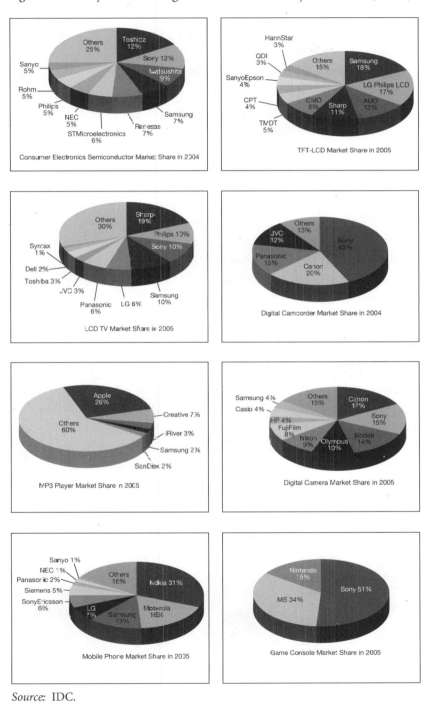

*Source:* IDC.

with 43% market share, and second in the digital camera sector, with 15% market share (Figure 1.4). Although Sony has traditionally not participated in the memory chip business (e.g., DRAMs), it has the second-largest market share in home appliance ASICs (Application-Specific Integrated Circuit).

### Entertainment

Morita believed that electronics hardware and software content such as music or film were complementary. He often commented that hardware and software content are two wheels of a cart. This is the reason that Sony initiated a joint venture with CBS Records in 1968, under the title of CBS Sony Records. Sony acquired the remaining share of CBS Records in 1988 for $2 billion and renamed the business Sony Music Entertainment. In 2004, it converted this business into a joint venture with BMG that is now called Sony BMG. In 1989, Sony acquired Columbia Pictures, a venerable film company that owned many valuable titles, for $6 billion. Its new name was Sony Pictures Entertainment.

At that time, Morita was thinking back to the disaster Sony suffered with its Betamax format since the late 1970s. Even though Sony's Betamax had a superior picture quality, Sony was outnumbered by the competing VHS (Video Home System) format, developed by JVC and Matsushita, which was favored by Hollywood because of its longer recording time. Sony finally gave up in 1988 when it began producing the VHS recorders. He believed that if Sony had owned an extensive video library and had introduced the Betamax-format videos earlier than its competitors did, Sony would have beaten JVC and Matsushita's VHS format in the standards war for video cassette recorders (VCRs). Morita's ego had suffered in this debacle, and he did not want to repeat the same mistake when Sony introduced a new recordable media, MiniDisc, and a next-generation video CD.

Although Sony Pictures had a couple of hits during its first few years such as *A League of Their Own* and *The Universal Soldier*, it also released numerous flops including *The Last Action Hero*, a $60 million extravaganza starring Arnold Schwarzenegger. Costs spiraled out of control. By 1994, Sony decided to resolve Sony Pictures' accumulated deficit of over $3.5 billion by writing off the goodwill portion of the initial purchase price. Sony Pictures later brought in a new management team and a new board of directors, and began a turnaround. In 2005, Sony acquired MGM's film library for $5 billion. As of 2006, Sony BMG trails only Universal in the music industry, holding 25% of market share, and Sony Picture Entertainment is now the biggest film company in the world, holding 40% of Hollywood's film assets.

*Games*

Sony's second-biggest hit has been PlayStation. In 1993, Sony established Sony Computer Entertainment as a joint venture between Sony and its Japanese subsidiary, Sony Music Entertainment, to oversee home gaming consoles and software. PlayStation was first released in 1994, and its market share rapidly increased. In 2000, PlayStation 2 was released with a DVD system as well as upgraded music and video features. These offerings have been very successful. By 2006, Sony had sold 100 million game platforms and 1 billion game cartridges.[16] Its portable PlayStation, PSP, can even access servers through a wireless connection. Sony is the clear market leader in the game business, with 51% market share. In 2006, Sony released PlayStation 3, which it equipped with its next-generation Blu-ray DVD player and a Cell chip, developed jointly with IBM and Toshiba.

*Network, IT, and Financial Business*

Although Sony's initial foray into home PCs in the early 1980s failed, Sony regrouped all its computer-related engineers in 1996 and set up a new company that developed a home multimedia computer called VAIO. This was not simply a PC or notebook but a machine that integrated a computer and AV (audiovisual). VAIO (video audio integrated operation) is a mixture of the sine curve of analogue and 0/1 values of digital. It also refers to the integration of AV and IT. Idei envisioned the VAIO as a platform for a network service over which Sony could offer an array of products. To this end, Sony also started Sonet, an Internet communication service in Japan that offers music downloads, e-commerce, and online financial services.

Sony's first attempt to enter the mobile communications market was unsuccessful, but it folded this business into a joint partnership with Ericsson in 2001. Sony-Ericsson is now tied with Samsung for third place in the mobile phone sector, and trails only Nokia and Motorola. Moreover, Sony established Sony Life Insurance jointly with Prudential in 1981, in an attempt to enter the financial service sector. In 2000, Sony opened Net Bank jointly with Sakura Bank and JP Morgan.

To sum up, Sony has diversified into many industries other than electronics, including music, motion pictures, games, mobile telecommunication, banking, and insurance. Roughly 40% of sales and profits were generated in the electronics business. The electronics business, however, has been Sony's bread-and-butter, contributing a stable income stream, while its other businesses have their ups and downs.

## Samsung Electronics

### A Humble Beginning

Samsung Electronics, a subsidiary of Samsung Group, was established in January 1969 with an investment of 330 million won. Samsung Group had begun with the founding of Samsung Corporation, a trading company, established by Byung-chull Lee in 1938. Since then, Samsung has diversified into foods, textiles, various financial services, petrochemicals, shipbuilding, heavy equipment, and aerospace. As of 2006, Samsung Group was a global conglomerate with 59 subsidiaries, $209 billion in total assets, $122 billion in sales, and 220,000 employees.

Samsung Group established Samsung Electronics in order to diversify into the electronics business. It began operations in 1970 by producing black-and-white TVs, an outdated product even at the time, simply because it did not have the technology to produce color TVs. In time, it began producing refrigerators, washing machines, color TVs, computer monitors, and microwaves. It vertically integrated by manufacturing electronic parts as it set up affiliates such as Samsung Corning, supplying glass for picture tubes; Samsung SDI, manufacturing TV tubes; and Samsung Electro-mechanics, manufacturing various other items.

Over time, Samsung Electronics' revenues grew significantly. Until the early 1990s, however, Samsung Electronics' home appliances were mainly OEM products, serving as loss leaders in large discount stores such as Sears, Wal-mart, and Kmart. While Samsung Electronics grew in terms of sales revenue, its products were still perceived as cheap and low-quality. For a long time, even in the TV business, where it enjoyed its largest sales, Samsung lacked the technology to produce expensive but more profitable large-sized or projection TVs. More recently, however, Samsung has become a leading producer of a wide array of appliances and consumer electronics. It currently is a market leader in LCD TVs, PDP (Plasma Display Panel) TVs, and color TVs.[17]

### Semiconductors and LCDs

Samsung Electronics' Semiconductor Division includes the memory business and the System LSI business, which makes nonmemory chips. Its memory business produces DRAMs, SRAMs (Static Random Access Memory), and flash memory, and has long been the commanding market leader in DRAM and SRAM. More recently, it has also become the market leader in flash memory. Since 1993, Samsung's dominance in memory businesses has never lost its number one position, and its market share is more than two times larger than that of the second-largest firm. It is also the most technologically innovative firm in these businesses.

The System LSI Division, which competes in nonmemory businesses, supplies products for home appliances, communication devices, and ASICs. This division is particularly strong in products that have a clear technological trajectory, and it focuses on System LSI products with substantial demand. It is weaker, however, in ASIC or SOC (solution on chip) businesses, which are characterized by many small application areas.

The LCD Division produces the LCD (Liquid Crystal Display) based on the TFT (Thin Film Transistor) technology, used for notebook PCs, monitors, and TVs. Samsung invested heavily in TFT technology early on, and has reaped substantial benefits from its initiative. In 2006, Samsung Electronics created a separate division for the LCD business. The LCD Division has also been operating a joint venture with Sony, called S-LCD, to produce seventh-generation LCD panels and is currently expanding the joint venture for the next generation. Samsung Electronics is currently the market leader in the LCD sector.

### Communication

Samsung entered the communications business in 1977 when it established Samsung GTE Communication jointly with GTE to produce electronic exchanges and transmission devices. Later, Samsung GTE Communication was merged into Samsung Semiconductor, and again into Samsung Electronics as a separate division in 1988. Until the mid-1990s, Samsung Electronics was an insignificant entity, even in Korea, way behind Motorola. A turning point for this division was the explosive growth of the market for second-generation digital mobile phones. The Korean government designated CDMA (Code Division Multiple Access) communication technology as the only standard for second-generation digital communication and prohibited redundant investment in the other standard, GSM (Global System for Mobile Communication). This step temporarily protected Samsung's domestic market and provided breathing room for Samsung to develop its technology. As the mobile phone market in Korea was deregulated, this division capitalized on Koreans' affinity for the latest technology by offering a variety of innovative phones and beating its competitors to market by introducing phones with cameras, MP3 players, and color displays. Currently, Samsung Electronics' mobile phones are its flagship product, enhancing its brand value, just as the Walkman elevated Sony into a globally-renowned brand. Samsung Electronics is the leading phone manufacturer in Korea and has been ranked third in worldwide market share since 2002.

## Sony and Samsung Electronics' Performance

### Sony's Stagnation

Figure 1.2 shows Sony's sales and profitability, as measured by operating income divided by sales. Sony's sales have been stagnant or trending downward since 2003. In addition, its profitability has declined since 1997. In 2006, Sony Group's overall profitability was 1%. As Figure 1.5 shows, Sony's poor performance mostly is the result of its audio and TV businesses. Audio has suffered dramatic drops in sales and profitability, and the TV sector has recently suffered substantial losses. Meanwhile, Sony's communication business became profitable only after Sony merged it into a joint venture with Ericsson. Overall, however, its game, film, and financial businesses have generally done well in recent years. Its music business, which lost money earlier in this decade, because of the increase in illegal downloads, has become more successful since Sony merged it into a joint venture with BMG and restructured it. Sony's traditional core businesses, audio and TV, with

*Figure 1.5*   Sales and Operating Incomes of Business Segments of Sony

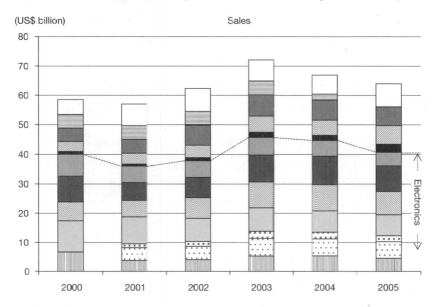

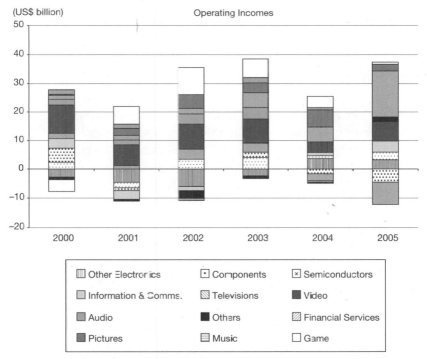

*Source:* Annual Report, Earnings Release.

their outstanding analog products such as the Walkman and Trinitron TV, have become less competitive, however, as these industries have embraced digital technology.

The reasons for Sony's long-term malaise are not completely clear. Why has a firm that is justly renowned for introducing many revolutionary products stumbled so badly during the last decade? Why has it been unable to respond successfully to major new technological developments such as the iPod and digital television?

Some reasons for Sony's troubles seem evident. First, Sony has not been able to release any new "wow" products, such as the Walkman, CD, handicams, or PlayStation, in recent years. Sony attempted to milk its Trinitron technology for too long, which created a legacy problem. Past success obstructed the future. It failed to invest early and aggressively in digital technology and flat-panel displays, which put it at a disadvantage relative to firms like Sharp and Matsushita. Sony may also have been constrained by its legacy products such as the MiniDisc and so failed to embrace a new digital music player. When asked whether Sony needs to hire more designers, engineers, or inventors to recapture the magic, Sony's newly appointed CEO, Howard Stringer, responded, "It's not about the absence of great engineers or the absence of great ideas. It's about the orchestration of the engineering groups and deploying them more effectively,"[18] hinting that some organizational deadweights may be responsible for its recent setback. According to a critic, "Sony continues to act like the great brand of yore, believing it can dream up products behind closed doors and unleash them on a grateful market at premium prices. This helps explain why Sony stuck with its Trinitron televisions long after flat-panel TVs had won the day. Moreover, Sony has a bias toward its home market. That's why its gadgets often feature complex software that Japanese love but that drives Americans crazy."[19]

Second, Sony has been preoccupied with obtaining synergies between hardware and content and has poured too much time and money into this elusive quest. "The synergy [between hardware and content] never got much further than Arnold Schwarzenegger using Sony Minidisc players in Sony's money-losing *The Last Action Hero*. Today at Sony, the word 'synergy' is taboo."[20] People wonder why Sony could not have come up with new products and services similar to Apple's iPod and iTunes, given its expertise in consumer electronics and its ownership of music and film content. Critics quickly pointed out that Sony's business divisions were so excessively individual that they were becoming silos, and no synergies were being created among the departments, even within its electronic businesses, not to mention between its electronic sector and the music and film sector. Even Chairman Stringer openly admits that Sony needs "better integration between our services and our device portfolio."[21] These explanations do have merit, but they fail to capture the underlying reasons why Sony's management has not responded more vigorously to these setbacks.

## The Rise of Samsung Electronics

Until the early 1990s, Samsung Electronics was an obscure Asian company that was known mainly for exporting cheap, generic OEM products. Recently, however, consumers have come to see Samsung Electronics' mobile phone as a high-end, high-performance product. Samsung's TVs and home electronics are also known for outstanding quality. Samsung is ranked first in memory semiconductors and is also rated highly in LCD monitors and LCD TVs. The media applaud Samsung's success, but have yet to explain how Samsung Electronics gained its strong position in such a short time.

The most commonly offered explanation is that Samsung Electronics identified key trends in the electronics industry and invested aggressively. In a nutshell, Samsung Electronics foresaw that semiconductors would be a crucial component that would impact many related sectors, and so it actively invested in this business. It also had good timing when it first picked up on the market shift from CRT to LCD and PDP. It then followed through and capitalized on this shift. Others argue that the Korean government's choice of the CDMA standard enabled Korean companies, including Samsung Electronics, to be first movers in CDMA technology. But these explanations beg several more fundamental questions. Most notably, how did Samsung Electronics identify these trends in the first place, and then how did it make the proper investments at the right time? What lessons, if any, can other companies learn from Samsung Electronics' example?

It is also unclear how Samsung Electronics can produce competitive and superior products. After all, it has about the same level of technological capability as its Japanese competitors. In some areas Samsung Electronics may even be inferior. In September 2004, a

*Figure 1.6*   Sales and Operating Income of Business Segments of Samsung
Electronics

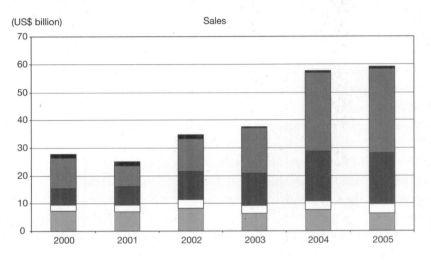

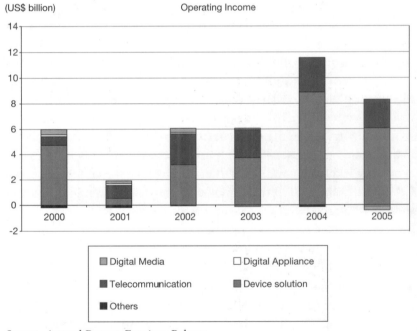

*Source:* Annual Report, Earnings Release.

senior official in a research institute at Itochu Corporation, one of the Japanese general trading companies, came to visit Samsung Electronics. He told a newspaper reporter that he was "not here to have a look at Samsung's technology," meaning that Samsung's technology was not superior to that of Japanese companies. He clarified his purpose of the visit: "I wonder why, although Samsung's overall technology level is still behind Japanese companies, how come the overall output is superior to theirs."[22] "When Samsung wants to get something done," says Intel Executive Vice President Sean M. Maloney, "the decision comes down from the top, and everybody moves at lightning-quick speed to just do it."[23] Samsung appears able to direct its capabilities so efficiently that it can produce products that most people would assume it should not be able to make at all. Other companies, whatever their business, need to learn how Samsung Electronics is able to do the impossible.

The performance of Samsung Electronics business divisions varies widely, however. Figure 1.6 shows the sales and operating profits of these divisions. Most of the profits come from two divisions—the Device Solution Division such as semiconductors and LCDs, and the Telecommunication Network Division. Other divisions, such as Digital Media and Digital Home Appliances, are not very successful. Even within the semiconductor business, Samsung Electronics does not do well in nonmemory semiconductor chips such as ASICs or microprocessors. If Samsung Electronics' outstanding performance originates from a core capability, why is the firm unable to extend this capability to nonmemory chips, digital media, and home appliances?

On top of that, most of Samsung Electronics' products are commodities or at least face the prospect of commoditization. The need to cut costs is constant, and the risk of fierce price competition always threatens. Also, most commodity businesses require large investments in production. Because sudden business fluctuations are inevitable, profits can drop dramatically. For example, the decreases in profitability during 1996 and 2001 (see Figure 1.2) reflect the price drop of DRAM, the source of a substantial percentage of Samsung Electronics' profit. Samsung Electronics has constantly attempted to diversify out of commodity businesses. But, as the glut of LCDs in 2006 demonstrates, these efforts have been only partially successful. Why does Samsung Electronics continue to remain vulnerable to these fluctuations?

## Strategy Content and Strategy Process

Traditionally, scholars in business strategy have studied either strategy content or strategy process. Studies of strategy content focus on what companies should do in order to secure competitive advantage. For example, strategy guru Michael Porter's industry analysis technique posits that a strategist should focus on an industry's characteristics, analyze the properties of an industry's structure and existing competition, and then formulate a firm's competitive strategy for that structure.[24] Unfortunately, the tendency to concentrate on strategy content typically leads to an artificial dichotomy between strategy formulation and implementation. It seems as though it's the CEO who analyzes the external environments of the company and formulates a strategy. All the lower lower-level managers do is implement the strategies the CEO has chosen. In reality, however, companies are not run so simply. Strategy formulation and implementation often go hand in hand. Even the best strategies are useless if nobody can carry them out.

In his analysis of the U.S. response during the Cuban missile crisis, Allison illustrated that the U.S. and Soviet responses were not perfectly orderly and based on rational choice, in which each side made a cool calculation of its opponent's nuclear armaments and decided that the risks of war were too great.[25] Instead decisions were really based on the routines of lower-level structures in the U.S. administration, specifically the State Department and Navy, and on the behind-the-scenes negotiations between President Kennedy and Chairman Khrushchev. In the end the Soviet Union pulled back its naval vessels and the U.S. agreed in return to withdraw its missiles in Turkey.[26]

The major decisions made by Sony and Samsung Electronics during the past decade did not simply originate from differences in these firms' strategic content. They were deeply rooted in their organizational processes and their executives' political behavior. In other words, the decision-making processes of these two companies can be understood only by accounting for rational, organizational, and political processes.

# Part 1 Strategic Analysis

# 2

# Prince and Pauper
# in the Analog World

There are only two ways for Sony to avoid being imitated by others; one is to set product standards on our own and the other is to have mechatronics, embodying our craftsmanship.

*—Norio Ohga, former CEO of Sony*[1]

Compared to other semiconductor products, the design technology of DRAMs is not so complicated, but the market for DRAMs is fairly large. We decided to focus all our resources in one product where we could do well. We had to take a lot of risks. In addition, fortune was on our side. The timing was great.

*—President Yeon-woo Lee,*
*Semiconductor Division of Samsung Electronics*[2]

As the Prince of the Analog world, Sony developed remarkable new products: the transistor radio, the Walkman, the camcorder, and the CD. It emphasized the creativity of its employees and made new product development its founding principle. On the other hand, Samsung Electronics was once merely an OEM company with limited technology and product development skills. It produced cheap, low-quality products by borrowing technology from overseas. But it succeeded in the DRAM business by aggressive investment, ruthless cost cutting, and focusing on new product development. It then applied these practices to similar products, such as flash memory and LCDs. These firms' initial conditions and early experiences have significantly affected how each company pursues new product development, as well as how they may have made different strategic choices in the face of the digital revolution.

## Sony, the Prince of Analog

### Founding Principles and New Product Development

All of Sony's management resources have been concentrated in the development of new products. Sony's capability to develop innovative products originated from the founding principles of the two founders, Ibuka and Morita, who set Sony's founding principle as "Freedom and Open-mindedness." They wished to contribute to society by providing new products to consumers that were based on a liberal, open corporate culture. Ibuka's speech at Sony's launching ceremony clearly shows this vision: "We can't beat big companies by imitating what they do. We must do something they can't. We don't have money or machines, but we have our brains and technologies. We can do almost anything with these two. We will not waste our brains and technologies in imitating what others do. Let's do something nobody has ever done before."[3]

Over time, the slogan of "Freedom and Open-mindedness" was even further instilled into Sony's corporate culture. Sony later developed various mottos for the employees, which were all varieties of this founding principle. Ibuka's favorite was to "know the new and pursue the new," instead of the old Chinese dictum "know the old and learn the new." Morita once claimed, "Markets don't exist, but are created."

From its very start, even people outside the company realized that Sony was extremely good at developing new products. In 1960, the *Weekly Asahi* carried an article by a Japanese journalist Soichi Ohya, who called Sony a "guinea pig." The main point of the article was that Sony had been treated like a guinea pig, used and wasted in the labs, so that other major electronics firms could copy its products and become dominant players.[4] Ibuka answered back that if the spirit of a guinea pig is to research new sectors and turn new ideas into new products, Sony would gladly be a guinea pig.[5] Ibuka's attitude, taking the expression "guinea pig" as a compliment rather than an insult, clearly demonstrates the importance of Sony's founding principle. Sony's employees later presented him with a golden guinea pig figurine.

Given Sony's emphasis on new product development that used proprietary technology, it is ironic that its first commercial success was a recorder. Wire recorders made of stainless steel wires had already existed before Sony began producing them. After World War II, Ibuka and Morita saw the U.S. military's tape recorders, and thought this product had a bright future.

At that time, Sony had no technology whatsoever. Sony's researchers had only a vague idea that they might need magnetic powder, and they tried scraping magnet bars for hours to extract powder, which they mashed into rice pigments and then covered with paper. After many experiments, as well as the purchase of a patented magnetic recording technology, Sony produced its first recorder, which weighed 45 kilograms, and was priced at 160,000 yen, an exorbitant price at that time. Not surprisingly, the recorder did not sell. Within a year, however, Sony introduced a new, improved recorder, which weighed only 13 kilograms, and began to develop the market.

Sony also developed its first major success, transistor radios, by licensing the transistor patent from Bell Labs. The only knowledge about transistors Sony had at that time was limited to a book called *Transistor Technology*, which Morita brought back from a business trip to the United States. Sony did not know how to produce transistors. The company dispatched an engineer, Kazuo Iwama, to visit U.S. factories, sketch various machines and devices he had seen throughout the day, and send them to Japan by mail. Sony persevered, using Iwama's drawings of machines to build its own equipment. In fact, Sony was not the first company to develop the transistor radio. A company called Regency, supported by Texas Instruments, introduced the first transistorized radio but failed to create a market. Eventually, Sony determined how to reduce the size of transistor radios radically, making them small enough to fit in a shirt pocket. It was a significant hit.

Similar successes followed through serendipity and determination. During the process of improving RCA's Shadow Mask technology, Sony accidentally discovered that the transmissibility of electronic rays increased when many fine lines were added to thin metal plates. This accidental discovery became the foundation for the Trinitron TVs' uniquely bright colors and high resolution screens. The Walkman was invented after Ibuka complained that the stereo recorder he carried during his overseas business trips was too big and heavy. When Morita instructed employees to remove the recording circuit and speakers from the existing recorder and replace them with a stereo amplifier, even Sony's engineers doubted whether any consumer would ever want such a product. But when the Walkman was released with only an earphone jack and a replay function, it became an unprecedented hit. In the 1980s, it commercialized CCDs (charge-coupled devices) and used them as a basis on which to manufacture digital cameras and camcorders.

Sony's key capability was not in breakthrough scientific discoveries, but in commercializing new, inexpensive, well-made products with large consumer potential that other companies neglected. It then found creative ways to market these offerings, even though other firms saw no future in them. Morita noted, "It is possible to have a good idea, a fine invention, but still miss the boat, so product planning, which means deciding how to use technology in a given market, demands creativity. And once you have a good product it is important to use creativity in marketing it. Only with these three kinds of creativity—technology, product planning, and marketing—can the public receive the benefit of a new technology. And without an organization that can work together, sometimes over a very long period, it is difficult to see new projects to fruition."[6]

### Relying on Internal Research and Development

Because Sony pursued innovative products, it geared its research and development toward this goal. As Figure 2.1 shows, Sony invests 6–7% of its sales in research and development. Yet it has concentrated on commercialization rather than developing fundamental scientific knowledge. Other companies had developed the source technologies for transistor radios, TVs, recorders, and CCDs, but Sony was quicker to commercialize them and package them into real products.[7] Sony had especially strong capabilities in miniaturization, aesthetically enhanced design, and manufacturing. Sony's commercialization capability relied entirely on internal research and development; it could not imitate

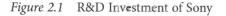

*Figure 2.1*   R&D Investment of Sony

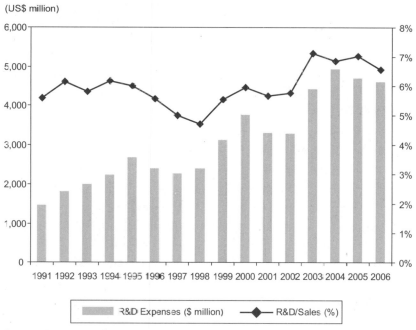

*Source:* Sony Annual Reports

others because it created products that had never existed before, and it relied on its own research centers for new product development. To facilitate product introductions, Sony's research and development organization created company-level and business-division-unit research centers, with a longer time horizon for development at the company level. In addition, Sony held technology strategy meetings in which divisional managers, researchers, and developers met to formulate research projects for each division, exchange information, and report on their R&D efforts.

Sony established a corporate culture that not only encouraged originality in research activities but even treated failures generously. Such a system was necessary to create products such as the Walkman, CDs, MiniDiscs, and PlayStation. Yet this system had its drawbacks. Costly failures were inevitable. Many researchers and developers also pursued their own fields of interest and used Sony's resources to develop technologies that were difficult to commercialize immediately.

## A Wide Range of Products

Samsung Electronics has focused on key parts such as semiconductors and LCD panels, but Sony has concentrated on developing final products for end users, and the scope of its offerings has been very wide. Sony's research and development team, however, has not set a specific direction for the future trajectories of the firm's technologies. As a result, technological development has typically occurred irregularly or accidently.

Sony has grown around its audio and video businesses (Figure 2.2). It has gradually added new capabilities in new product areas, such as computers, and has looked for opportunities in new businesses such as music, film, and games. Because Sony created new products for customers in a variety of fields, it developed a wide array of technologies on its own. Sony's Aibo, a robot dog, is a good example of such far-flung R&D efforts.

Sony also has a sizable parts manufacturing business; Figure 1.5 shows its Semiconductor and Components Division, which sells parts and intermediate goods and represents about 18% of Sony's overall sales. If internal sales were included, the size of Sony's parts business would be larger. Yet unlike Samsung Electronics, Sony's focus on producing parts has been primarily for internal use.

Because it pursued new product development, it often could not source parts externally. For example, Sony needed to make storage devices such as memory sticks, long-lasting compact batteries, and color displays and CCDs for its camcorders and digital cameras. Furthermore, internal sourcing is sometimes crucial in achieving a greater functionality of its products. "A manufacturer who's purchasing all of these components from outside could never achieve such a thin body," declared a head of product planning for digital cameras.[8]

As a consequence of all these trends, Sony finds itself thinly stretched with too many products while being targeted by too many rivals. According to Stringer, "Unlike almost any other company, we are in every area. You have Kodak and Canon on the camera side. You have Dell and HP on the computer side. You have Philips, the Chinese, Samsung knocking on the door on the TV side. Effectively, Sony is battling on a very broad front. That may be one way to do it, but you're going to have to look at the balance sheet to see if there are too many winners and losers this way."[9]

*Figure 2.2* Sony's New Products and Its Stock Prices

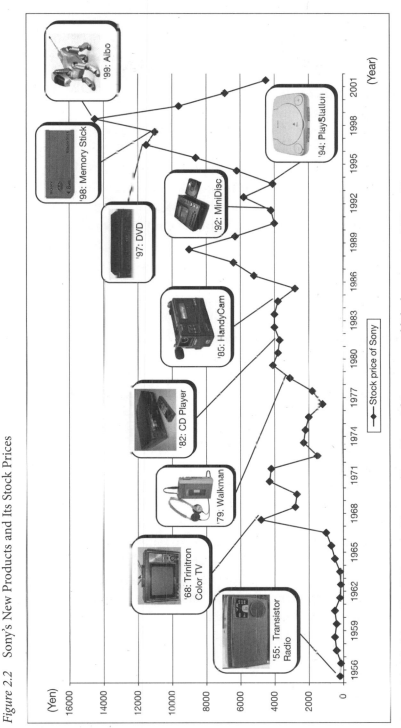

*Source:* Modified from Iba, T. From the History of Sony Financial Strategy, unpublished manuscript, 2003, p. 31.

**Obsession with Its Own Standards**

Sony has frequently attempted to establish its own technology as the industry standard. Sometimes it has succeeded. It developed the standard for CDs jointly with Philips and reaped substantial rewards.[10] It chose not to make PlayStation compatible with the cartridges of Nintendo and Sega, then the two largest video game firms, and became the industry leader. Trinitron was another of Sony's original and unique technologies.

At other times, these efforts have failed, most notably in its attempt to dominate the emerging VCR market by developing the high-performance Betamax VCR. Betamax lost out to JVC's VHS system, which became the de facto standard. In the late 1990s, Sony tried to replicate its success in CDs when it joined with Philips again to make its Multimedia CD the industry standard. This effort met fierce resistance; the product had a smaller capacity than the SD-method DVD, developed by Matsushita and Toshiba. Finally, only after it became likely that the SD-method DVD would become the industrial standard, did Sony compromise with Toshiba and Matsushita on a unified standard for DVDs.[11] More recently, Sony's Blu-ray format for high-definition DVDs, jointly developed with Matsushita, News Corp., Samsung Electronics, and Disney, won the standard battle against the HD DVD format, which Microsoft, GE's NBC Universal, Toshiba supported.

As the story of Betamax suggests, Sony's strong preference for owning unique standards is risky. It is costly to create standards, and Sony has lost a lot of money when its standards have not won out because consumers who care about compatibility have hesitated to buy Sony's products. It is also costly to maintain its own standard. For instance, Sony had to vertically integrate into picture tube manufacturing for its Trinitron TV, which was not compatible with other external sources. The pricey Blu-ray DVDs, installed in PlayStation 3, became one of the factors for the console's delay and high price, which eventually depressed its sales. In addition, Sony's obsession with its own standards have biased it against other firms' technologies or standards when these were incompatible with its own. This is the NIH (not-invented-here) syndrome. At times, Sony's efforts to develop new products, when it instead needs to work with other firms, have been inhibiting because it is swimming against the industry tide.

## The Late-Starter, Samsung Electronics

### Relying on Borrowed Technologies

Samsung Electronics had no technological capability when it was first established in 1969. When it visited Japanese TV manufacturers in 1974 and asked them to supply picture tubes for color TVs, these firms told Samsung Electronics that even if it tried to offer technical know-how, the company was probably too far behind to absorb any of the technologies it was offered.[12] Finally, Samsung Electronics succeeded in persuading Matsushita Electric to sell it color TV picture tubes and was able to start production.

Until the late 1970s, Samsung Electronics was capable of nothing more than assembly, and it imported all its key components from Japanese suppliers. When it began producing its own goods, many were of extremely poor quality. Samsung Electronics produced an electric fan, but it was so poorly designed and manufactured that merely lifting it up with one hand broke its neck. This defect would now be perceived as a serious problem, but at that time, people at Samsung just assumed that "electronics products are complicated, so it is natural for them to break down a lot." Gradually, however, it began improving its production capabilities, often by purchasing them from other firms. For instance, it secured technology and production facilities for microwave products by acquiring a U.S. company named Ampherex that produced a key part called the magnetron. As a consequence, its microwaves became a flagship export item for a considerable time. Samsung also secured production technologies by acquiring private exchanges, jointly developed by GTE and KIST.

### Success in the DRAM Business

A turning point for Samsung Electronics was its entry into the semiconductor business. Originally, Samsung had grown interested in the semiconductor business during the oil crisis in 1973 when it became difficult to secure semiconductors from Japanese companies. Without a stable supply of semiconductor components, Samsung's TV and refrigerator production facilities had to stop, which caused huge scheduling problems. The opportunities associated with semiconductors were obvious, but all the leading firms in the industry were from Japan or the United States. Korean semiconductor firms were capable only of assembling OEM products, and when foreign firms such as Motorola or Fairchild entered the Korean market, they refused to transfer any technology. Moreover, the industry required huge upfront investment in production facilities, which gave potential entrants pause.

In 1974, Samsung's founder Byung-chull Lee acquired Korea Semiconductor, an almost bankrupt company, and ventured into the semiconductor business. Soon afterward, Samsung Semiconductor faced huge challenges due to its lack of technical know-how and quality problems. Samsung produced chips for electronic watches, but had poor market timing. It also produced transistors in 1977 through reverse engineering, but even its own business divisions did not want to use them. By the late 1970s, it was almost out of business. Lee saved the company by bringing in Japanese semiconductor engineers to transfer technology to his own engineers, improving production facilities, and reorganizing Samsung Semiconductor's technical workforce. At that time, planes going to Korea from Japan on Saturday mornings and back to Japan on Sunday evenings were full of these moonlighting engineers. An implicit agreement among them was not to ask each other what they did during the weekend.[13]

After the business was stabilized in the early 1980s, Lee decided to enter the VLSI (Very Large Scale Integration) semiconductor businesses even though his firm was ill-equipped to do so. After refining his business plan, he chose to specialize in memory, despite being advised against this idea, because he believed that it would be easier to start with general-purpose technologies such as memory, and he also believed that the demand for memory chips would surely rise in the future as the information industry grew. He selected DRAMs, because of all memory products, economies of scale were the most important in this area. He built factories in Giheung.

In the semiconductor business, timing is crucial. Life cycles are short, and demand is volatile. Further, DRAMs have the shortest life cycle among all products with a similar level of integration (see Figure 2.3); DRAM prices drop by over 80% within 1–2 years of a product's initial run. The DRAM business offers high risk and high return, and firms competing in it can win big or quickly go bankrupt.

When it first entered the industry, Samsung Electronics bought 64K DRAM technology from Micron, which was financially distressed at the time. While Samsung Electronics learned about this technology,

Figure 2.3 DRAM Generations and Prices

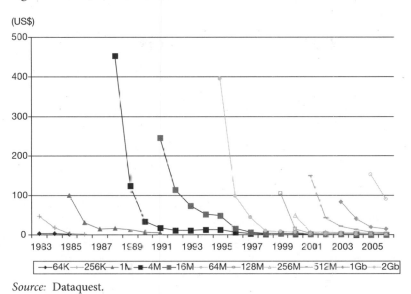

(US$)

Source: Dataquest.

it began to develop 256K DRAMs. To do so, Samsung brought in highly-trained researchers and engineers and paid them four to five times as much as the then president of the firm was receiving. Most of them were Koreans, schooled in the United States and with work experience in U.S. semiconductor firms.[14] It established a U.S. subsidiary with an R&D center and prototype production facilities and had these personnel train promising young Korean engineers. After these engineers returned to Samsung Semiconductor's Korean facilities they worked night and day; in product development they soon surpassed their U.S. counterparts.[15]

Through such arduous effects, Samsung released the 64K DRAM in September 1984, but quickly faced a serious crisis due to the plunge in 64K DRAM prices from $4 in early 1984 to $.30 in 1985. Samsung's manufacturing cost was $1.30 per unit, so it lost about a dollar for every DRAM it sold. Samsung Semiconductor had cumulative losses of $300 million by 1986; once again, its equity capital was depleted.

During this recession, Intel and several other U.S. DRAM producers gave up their DRAM businesses entirely. Japanese firms also cut back their capital expenditures and production capacity. Yet Samsung was determined to succeed in DRAM production; it added capacity and continued developing 256K DRAMs. By mid-1987, it had finally succeeded.

In 1987, Samsung's investment in DRAMs started to pay off. That year, the U.S. government raised an anti-dumping suit against Japanese semiconductor manufacturers. In the wake of this accusation, the U.S. government and Japanese manufacturers reached a voluntary export restraint agreement, and Japanese manufacturers accordingly cut back their exports to the United States. Soon afterward, the price of DRAMs began to rise. Demand for the 256K DRAM grew especially rapidly, but Japanese producers had already reduced their 256K production lines and had shifted much of their manufacturing capacity to the 1M DRAMs, believing that the 256K production lines were outdated. In contrast, Samsung's main DRAM product remained the 256K chip. Samsung's profits surged. In 1988, Samsung's profits were large enough to offset all its cumulative losses. In fact, Samsung's investment in manufacturing facilities in 1987 contributed to its success in the semiconductor boom, which continued into the early 1990s. This success was possible because the management believed that only by investing during recessions could the company reap great profits during the boom period.

By the early 1990s, Samsung had become the most competitive DRAM producer; in 1993, it held the largest market share. Soon after it achieved this milestone, it also became the industry's technological leader. When Japanese producers introduced the 4M DRAM, Samsung was only slightly behind. Samsung caught up to Japanese producers with the introduction of the 16M DRAM, and surpassed them with the introduction of the 64M DRAM. Samsung has continued to maintain this lead through its production of the first Giga DRAM chip.

Samsung Electronics was faster than other firms in time-to-market because it not only increased its R&D investment but also pursued a "parallel development strategy" in which it initiated the development for next-generation products such as 64M and 256M DRAMs while developing and mass producing the current generation.[16] This strategy accelerated new product development and enabled new technologies to be directly applied to next-generation products. In addition, Samsung Electronics began using the parallel development method to other related memory products, such as flash memory, thus accelerating the development speed of all its products.

## Production Process Technology

The R&D and production departments within Samsung Electronics' Semiconductor Division closely interacted to improve production yields. They avoided the traditional, sequential approach of having the process engineers come in only after design was completed and having the test engineer take over after the production process was done. Instead, Samsung forces engineers from design and manufacturing to work together in order to solve the numerous technical problems in product development and mass production.[17] Samsung Electronics has also developed a system that can estimate the yield from the pilot development stage by integrating the development and production processes. It has built an internal knowledge-sharing system in which detailed information collected during development and production processes are stored, and it assigns more than half the engineers who had worked on existing lines to build new ones, thus enabling knowledge-sharing between existing and new lines.

Further, Samsung Electronics continuously promotes process innovations that enhance productivity, even after the mass-production phase is initiated. For instance, it narrowed the widths of 16M DRAM circuits from 0.42 μm to 0.35 μm, a circuit width originally designed for 64M DRAMs. By applying finer circuits into the same size wafer, the size of the chip can be reduced to less than half its original size, and consequently the number of chips produced out of one wafer can be more than doubled. This progress of so-called shrinking production technology has been especially useful for increasing chips' stability and applicability in mobile products.

## Focus on Technologies with Clear Trajectories

Using the capabilities it gained with DRAMs, Samsung Electronics has expanded into other business areas, such as flash memory and LCDs. A flash memory is a kind of memory that does not lose information even if electricity is disconnected. The production process for it is similar to that for DRAMs, and the production lines for the two can be shared. Similarly, because each pixel in an LCD is a transistor itself, the LCD production process is also much like that for DRAMs. Likewise, flash memories and LCDs all have industrial standards, as do DRAMs, and are commodities that can be produced with general-purpose technologies. Unlike Sony, which has focused on producing unique and differentiated products, Samsung Electronics has produced commodities, but has sought competitive cost advantages.

Not surprisingly, the technological and product portfolios of Samsung Electronics are very different from Sony's. Samsung Electronics invests in technologies that have clear trajectories with clear evolutionary progress and industrial standards. Even late-comers can succeed in such businesses. Also, Samsung has taken Moore's Law to heart, the principle that states that the degree of integration doubles every eighteen months, by doubling its efforts in R&D to develop new products according to this schedule. This effort provided a very simple and unified goal for all Samsung employees. For example, because the 256M DRAMs would be the next-generation DRAMs within 18 months after 128M DRAMs, the only mandate would be to develop 256M DRAMs within 18 months, having all its employees committed on this single goal.

Similar trends exist in many of Samsung Electronics' other businesses. For instance, there is a trend called "Hwang's Law" in the flash memory sector, named after President Chang-Kyu Hwang of

*Figure 2.4*    Sony and Samsung Electronics' Patents (1986–2006)

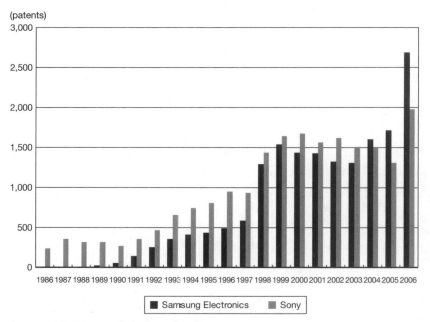

*Source:*  U.S. Patent and Trademark Office.

Samsung's Semiconductor Division, which states that the degree of integration doubles annually. In other areas, such as mobile phones, Samsung has become expert at rapidly adding new features (such as cameras and MP3 players), miniaturizing technology, and reducing costs. As a result, the life cycle of mobile phones has become shorter and shorter, just like that of DRAMs. Similarly, LCDs have a clear technological development, increasing the panel size while improving its yields.

In short, Samsung Electronics has invested in businesses for which it could have the highest returns given its resource level, and unlike Sony, it has not hesitated to source technology from other firms and other countries. It has been only in the last 15 years that Samsung Electronics has begun to develop technologies in-house. Figure 2.4 shows the number of U.S. patents obtained by Samsung Electronics and Sony over time. In 1986, Samsung Electronics had only one U.S. patent, and Sony had 240. The number of U.S. patents held by Samsung Electronics began to explode in the 1990s, however, and exceeded those held by Sony in 2004. Nonetheless, most of Samsung Electronics' patents were in semiconductor-related areas. Of course, U.S. patents show an incomplete picture of the technologies Sony and Samsung Electronics own, and each may possess other technologies and core capabilities that it has not patented. Certainly, as shown in Figure 2.5, the R&D investment of Samsung Electronics is but a fraction

*Figure 2.5*   Samsung Electronics' R&D Expenses

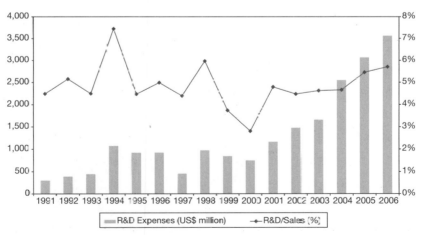

*Source:* Korea Investors Service

of Sony's, as shown in Figure 2.1. Samsung Electronics has had a much higher patent-to-investment ratio than Sony has precisely because it has focused its R&D efforts in technologies with clear trajectories. Its focus on general-purpose technology has let it concentrate on swift new product development and production efficiency, despite its deficiency in technological know-how. In contrast, Sony invested sizable sums in a wide range of technological areas in order to develop new products. Strategy is about focusing resources to generate competitive advantage. In this regard, Samsung Electronics is an exemplary strategic firm.

# 3

# Digital Dream Kids
# and
# the Digital Sashimi Shop

Sony adopted the concept of "Digital Dream Kids," which expresses Sony's desire to utilize digital technologies to create unique, fun products that fulfill the dreams of customers who have grown up in the digital age. Making the most of the seemingly limitless potential of digital technologies, Sony's staff will strive to become bright-eyed Digital Dream Kids themselves, drawing on the many audiovisual technologies that Sony has developed over the years to create new products and new markets for the digital age.

*—Nobuyuki Idei, former CEO of Sony*[1]

Speed is the key to all perishable commodities from sashimi to mobile phones. Even expensive fish becomes cheap in a day or two. For both the sashimi shop and the digital industry, inventory is detrimental and speed is everything.

*–Jong-yong Yun, CEO of Samsung Electronics*[2]

The sizable gap between Sony's and Samsung Electronics' technology level and new product development capabilities began to narrow as the industry moved from analog to digital technology. In the age of digital technologies, industry standards often exist, and all necessary technologies tend to be concentrated in one chip set. Therefore, as long as the same parts are used, all end products should be of roughly equal quality. In this regard, digital technology is a "disruptive technology" because it eliminates qualitative differences among end products.[3] Sony and Samsung Electronics have pursued somewhat different paths to meet this challenge. Sony has emphasized its network and has continued promoting the development of new products and services. Samsung Electronics has leveraged its strengths in semiconductors to focus on other related components.

## Digital Revolution

### Shifts in Competitive Advantages

In the mid-1990s, the global electronics industry rapidly converted from analog to digital technology. In digital technology, analog signals are transformed into signs of 0 and 1 before being transmitted. Breakthroughs in techniques for detecting and correcting various transmission errors dramatically improved the quality of digitally transmitted data. LP records and CDs are good examples that clearly demonstrate the difference between analog and digital technologies.

LPs record sounds in the shape of grooves on record plates, and a needle detects the miniscule changes in the grooves. In CDs, fine holes that indicate 0 or 1 are engraved on silver plates, and a laser detects them to replay the sound. LPs deteriorate in sound quality due to storage conditions and replaying, but music stored on CDs can be perfectly replayed almost indefinitely.

Other examples that characterize the digital technology include convergence and broadband. Convergence denotes the merging of various devices that were once distinct. Broadband involves the instantaneous transmission of massive amounts of digital information via high-speed Internet. For example, people used to listen to music stored on CD players, but they can now save music in MP3 file formats, play it on media such as computers or iPods, and share files with others in real-time via online sharing sites.

With these developments, the electronics industry faces commoditization and modularization, and the lifecycle of electronics products has become shorter.[4] In the analog era, the technological gap between Sony and Samsung Electronics was insurmountable. Circuit technology was crucial, and the experience and accumulated know-how of engineers were pivotal to enhancing product quality. A late entrant such as Samsung Electronics could not dream of catching up with Sony or Philips. It was also possible to maintain a monopoly on some technologies during the analog era. Sony's Trinitron technology was patent-protected, and it was virtually impossible for other competitors to access it. In the digital age, however, technologies are concentrated on one chip-set, so there are no differences in quality if industry players purchase the same chip-set. Thus, digital technology nullifies all technical gaps when one inventor standardizes a technology. For example, MP3 became the de facto standard for music source files. Manufacturers of digital music players take the format as given, and design and manufacture products using the MP3 chip. Because international organizations such as the International Standards Organization or Institute of Electrical and Electronics Engineers determine the industrial standards for various digital technologies, it is growing more difficult for one company to monopolize a standard.

Second, modularization means that the value chain of a product is divided into more or less independent modules. Architectural innovation determines the conditions for modularization, defines how a system comprising a product is divided into numerous modules, and determines how these modules are interconnected.[5] Because modularization reduces the interactions among each module, it lowers the cost of switching parts or modifying the value chain. It makes changes within each module easier, thus promoting innovation and technological development, and specialization within modules enables firms to reap scale economies. It lowers production costs, yet improves product performance. PCs (personal computers) are the exemplar of modularization. In the PC industry, firms typically specialize in one module, such as Intel in microprocessors, Microsoft in operating systems, and Seagate in hard drives.

Third, in the digital era, product life cycles have become shorter. New models of PCs with faster CPUs (Central Processing Unit), more RAM (Random Access Memory), and larger hard drives are released every few months. As a result, the price of old models rapidly drops, and new products can command premium prices for only a brief period. Companies that are late in releasing new products cannot recoup their product development costs because the prices for these products have already dropped.

This trend is compounded by the convergence of different products. For example, TVs and PCs used to be drastically different products, but they now share several common features because of digitalization. As Figure 3.1 suggests, digital TVs are more similar to PCs than they are to analog TVs in terms of software program sizes and transistor intensity. Further, as digital TVs have become more technologically similar to PCs, the nature of these businesses increasingly overlaps; the commoditization, shortened product life cycle, horizontal specialization, and modularization that have long characterized the PC industry are now more apparent in the digital TV industry. This means that companies need to adopt strategies for digital TVs that are different from the ones they used for analog TVs.

According to Clayton Christensen, author of the *Innovator's Dilemma*, digital technology is a disruptive innovation. Based on his study of technological innovation in the hard drive industry, Christensen argued that industry incumbents respond well to gradual innovation such as technology for improving productivity, but they usually are not successful in addressing the challenges of disruptive innovations. And this make them fall behind.[6] At Sony, ownership of standards and skill in miniaturization once helped it achieve competitive advantage, but today these advantages are far less relevant than they once were.[7] As a result, Sony has recently been losing its competitive advantage in strategic components. The magnetic drum technology once used in VCRs is not useful in the age of DVDs, and Trinitron CRTs have little

*Figure 3.1*    Convergence of TVs and PCs

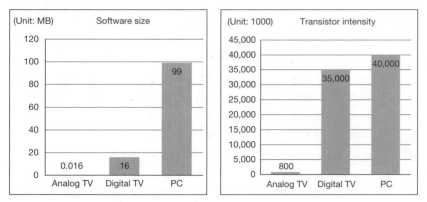

*Source: Diamond Weekly*, February 12, 2005, p. 43.

value in the age of LCD TVs. Even DVDs have become obsolete as the industry moves toward flash memory, which uses no disc or device.

In contrast, Sony has been weak in digital technology, particularly in the IT and network fields; its technological lead in the digital realm was restricted to stand-alone digital audio and video such as CDs or DVDs. In addition, Sony has relatively little of the architectural competence necessary to design a platform upon which many different types of products can be developed. But this is now a critical skill in creating digital products. In contrast, the advent of the digital era has given late entrants like Samsung Electronics a good opportunity to catch up with the incumbents.

**Two Different Approaches**

Because digitalization enables specialization and standardization, it increases competition and puts downward pressures on prices and profitability.[8] There are two ways for firms to respond to these trends. One involves "endless innovation" of new products and services in order to avoid the commodity trap. This was Sony's strategy. Sony's efforts to diversify into the entertainment business were motivated by the same desire.

The alternative strategy, which Samsung Electronics adopted, starts with an open acknowledgement of commoditization. Jong-yong Yun of Samsung Electronics has a special interpretation of this trend. To use his phrase, the "Digital Sashimi Theory" posits that "Speed is the key to all perishable commodities from sashimi to mobile phones. Even expensive fish becomes cheap in a day or two. For both the sashimi shop and the digital industry, inventory is detrimental and speed is everything."[9] Unless a firm comes up with its products quicker than its competitors, it is doomed to the hellish competition of commodities. Just as it did with DRAM production, Samsung Electronics has aggressively invested in product and process technology so that it can beat its competitors to market and capture price premiums before its offerings become commodities.

These two paths also coincide with the norm of the electronics industry, which is often dubbed the "smile curve." This curve refers to profitability levels at different parts of the value chain, namely core parts, assembly, and service. At the beginning and end of the value chain, core parts and service reap high profit, but profitability

*Figure 3.2*    Value Chain of the Electronics Industry and Two Responses

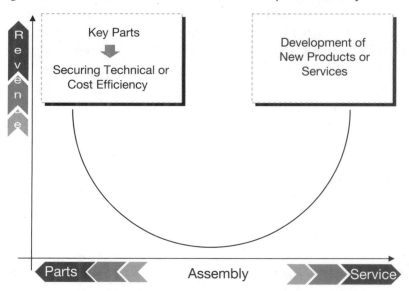

in assembly (that is, the middle of the value chain) is low. In the PC business, for instance, the profitability of firms such as Microsoft and Intel, which manufacture core components, tends to be very high, whereas assemblers' profitability is very low (see Figure 3.2).

Only manufacturers such as Dell that do not carry inventory can fully capitalize on the frequent price decreases of components. Meanwhile, subsequent to its merger with Compaq, HP adopted strategies that reinforced its service capability, believing it could provide differentiated services to consumers. In electronics, Sony's network strategy has involved investments in games, music, and film, which are not commodities. Conversely, Samsung Electronics has strictly adhered to its original strategy of investing and pursuing cost advantages in core parts such as flash memory and LCDs.

## Sony's Digital Dream Kids

### Idei's Network Strategy
Soon after Idei became Sony's president in 1995, he began advocating "regeneration" for Sony. Consistent with Sony's founding principles of freedom, open-mindedness, dynamism, and originality, he promoted

his "Digital Dream Kids" catchphrase to demonstrate Sony's will to "utilize digital technologies to create unique, fun products that fulfill the dreams of customers who have grown up in the digital age."[10] More specifically, this phrase signified that Sony would pursue appropriate business strategies for the digital age in all of its business areas, encompassing hardware such as AV devices, and software, including film, music, and games. And so it would provide consumers with products they had dreamed of. With the advent of the digital and network age, Idei also attempted to develop network services such as the Internet, e-commerce, and broadcasting in order to help Sony create greater synergy between its hardware and software assets.

Sony's strategy was to actively respond to the digital revolution. "Today, the markets for entertainment hardware and software are being redefined by the forces of digital and networking technologies. Moreover, the advent of digital satellite broadcasting and other types of electronic distribution is enhancing the value of all types of entertainment software. Sony's course of action is clear. We are emphasizing information technology as a key element in the company's future business development. We will continue to promote the incorporation of digital technology in our hardware and software businesses. Information technology will also add value to our vast store of music and filmed entertainment assets. As this process unfolds, we believe it is critical that we extend our business domain to encompass broadcasting and other forms of electronic distribution."[11]

Idei highlighted information technology because it became easier to create synergy between hardware and software content as Internet and broadband technology developed. This synergy was difficult to achieve in the analog age because music and film content were packaged and delivered separately in different media such as CDs or VCRs. In the digital age, however, all such content is composed, stored, and shared real-time in digitalized formats. Mergers such as AOL and Time Warner or Disney and ABC at that time shared similar strategic intent to create new value by distributing digitalized contents through networks.

Idei created the VAIO computer in 1996 in order to execute his network strategy. He believed VAIO would be an important conduit for the digital distribution network. Sony's VAIO-branded super-slim computers, released in 1997–1998, were super-popular, at one point enjoying a domestic market share of 60%. Sony then entered the broadcasting business by purchasing 25% of JSkyB satellite digital broadcasting business in 1997. At the same time, it created a protocol called HAVi (home audio video interoperability) for networking among all of its home electronics products, and attempted to construct a home network system that connected these products. Sony implemented the IEEE 1394 standard and created i.Link, an interface between A&V products and PCs, and implemented this interface in digital camcorders and VAIO computers. Sony also developed Aperios, an original OS (operating system) for home appliance products, and installed it in digital set-top boxes.

Sony also started digitizing its film and music content in preparation for the broadband age. According to Sony's 2002 annual report, it had already digitized 1,000 films, 33,000 hours of TV programs, and 500,000 songs.[12] Sony also established Movielink jointly with four other film companies, Pressplay jointly with Universal, and its own EverQuest site. It announced plans to use these sites for online downloads of Sony's films, music, and games, respectively.

Yet Idei's grand vision went unrealized. *BusinessWeek* observed: "Sony is betting on the networked universe—the fusion of Sony digital devices with content, all transmitted at the blink of an eye through high-speed connections, both wired and wireless. But this future has yet to arrive. A crucial experiment in wireless data phones went seriously awry. Devices envisioned as portals to the Net or to other digital formats, such as the PlayStation, have yet to play this role in any serious way. Even so, it's an alluring vision…. Sony managers have been preaching about this glorious networked future for half a decade with little to show for it. The company, in short, is caught between a past that no longer works and a future that hasn't arrived."[13] Problems in Sony's core business areas—digital TVs, digital audio, and PlayStation—prevented Sony from executing this vision.

### Flat Panel Displays: Investment Decision

While Idei promoted the development of digital products with the Digital Dream Kids strategy, Sony was having a hard time transitioning from analog Trinitron CRT-based TVs to PDP or LCD-based digital TVs. Sony had hesitated to invest in flat panel TVs. It had further reinforced its long-standing dominance in analog TV when it introduced WEGA in 1997, and was reluctant to embrace next-generation technology when the current generation was so profitable. WEGA symbolized the apex for analog Sony, as it applied flat CRT technology and solved the problem of distorted images near the edges of the screen. It was extremely popular with consumers. Ironically, Sony had been proactive in developing digital display technologies. In fact, Sony developed the Plasmatron flat panel display jointly with a U.S. firm, Tektronix, as early as in 1996. Yet although Sony believed that the transition from CRTs to flat panels was inevitable, it did not invest in production facilities for PDPs or LCDs because it believed such an investment was strategically unwise. In other words, it was a deliberate strategic choice—not a legacy problem—not to invest in flat panel displays.

President Ando responded to repeated questions by analysts about why Sony was not investing in PDPs or LCDs: "The success of our growth strategy depends above all on accelerating our network strategy. Sony sells four network gateway products: TVs, PCs, mobile devices such as mobile phones, and PS2. We supply many other electronics products that connect to these gateways. This is Sony's strength, and it is essential to take a comprehensive approach to all these products so that we can devise methods to add still more value. Hardware does not add value on its own. . . . In terms of our device strategy, people outside of Sony sometimes ask whether the fact that we do not manufacture LCDs and PDPs for TV use in-house is a weakness. However, we have a plan to ensure a reliable, long-term supply of these two display panels."[14] Idei also asserted: "In regards to flat panel displays, I believe that Sony needs to develop a technology that is unquestionably superior to CRT [cathode ray tube televisions], is of high quality and is able to produce light on its own. Not having PDP and LCD production capabilities is a *strength* [emphasis added] of Sony and is the reason why we did not invest in them."[15]

Sony's senior managers believed that PDPs and LCDs were commodities that could be more efficiently supplied by external sources, and instead focused on developing organic light-emitting displays (OLED), which they believed would be the dominant future display format. In contrast, Sharp invested heavily in LCDs, Panasonic in PDPs, and Samsung Electronics in both PDPs and LCDs.[16]

Sony's decision not to invest in PDPs or LCDs cost it dearly. Demand for these products exploded in 2002, as several firms introduced PDP and LCD TVs and priced them aggressively (see Figure 3.3).[17] President Ando confessed: "The switch from CRTs to flat panel displays came too soon, much sooner than we expected." Sony, which relied on external sources such as NEC, fell to third in the market and suffered greatly from the shortage of flat panels. Further, Sony found it difficult to commercialize OLED technology for many technical reasons. Corporate Vice President Kutaragi openly admitted: "We [Sony] made a mistake in transition."[18] Eventually, Sony set up a joint venture with Samsung Electronics, S-LCD, in 2003 in order to secure a reliable supply of flat panels. "Kutaragi had to convince Sony executives that it had to tie up with Samsung if it wanted to get enough panels at a low enough cost."[19] In 2005, Sony agreed to expand this joint venture, and invested an additional $2 billion to build large LCD flat panels.

Sony's initial failure to invest reflects several more problems beyond legacy issues. First, as noted before, Sony has a strong NIH (not-invented-here) syndrome, and has typically avoided investing in technologies it has not developed itself. It might have avoided investment in commodity-type flat panels such as LCDs and PDPs

*Figure 3.3*    Transition from CRTs to Flat Panel Displays

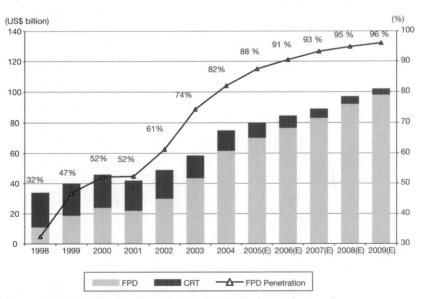

*Source:* Hsieh, D. Flat Panel Display Market Outlook. DisplaySearch, November 5, 2005.

that its competitors such as Sharp or Matsushita had developed, and instead tried to develop its own display such as OLEDs. Second, Sony had invested heavily in CRT TV factories, including a huge TV assembly plant in Pittsburgh in 1993 and, in a joint venture with Corning and Asahi, another huge factory for CRT glass in 1997. Sony expected that it would not recoup the investment for at least ten years.[20] And so Sony had a strong incentive to recoup the investment by operating the factories as long as possible, inevitably postponing its investment in flat panels.

## Confusions around Digital Music Players

Why did Sony fail to develop a digital music player similar to Apple's iPod? Sony was the natural candidate to invent such a device because it had done so repeatedly with the Walkman, CD, DVD, and MiniDisc. Moreover, Sony owned a vast amount of music. In fact, Sony had planned a new digital music player long before Apple introduced the iPod, and presented two new digital music players at Comdex in 1999. One was the Memory Stick Walkman, which enabled users to store music files in Sony's storage device, the memory stick. The other was called the VAIO Music Clip, which had a built-in memory. These devices stored digital music files in storage devices, and directly read and replayed them without discs or tapes, unlike existing analog music players. Also, they allowed sharing music with PCs, a type of digital convergence.

Unfortunately, these two new digital music players received unfavorable reviews, both internal and external. And because two of Sony's business divisions, the Personal Audio Company and the VAIO Company, had developed these products separately without any cooperation or communication, Sony now had two devices that were both inferior to Apple's iPod rather than one device that combined the strength of these two divisions. Sony released Networkman, a product similar to iPod, in 2004, only after iPod had become extremely successful and MP3 players had become mainstream products.

Several factors further limited Networkman's success. Most notably, because Sony owned a music business and was far more sensitive to illegal copying and sharing of digital music files than Apple was, it made Networkman incompatible with the MP3 format. This approach contrasts with that of Apple, which allowed files downloaded from its online music site, iTunes, to be replayed by iPods only, but did not prevent consumers from playing their own MP3 format files with iPods. Sony's VAIO Company and Personal Audio Company also released VAIO Pocket and the Network Walkman almost simultaneously, which added to customer confusion. In addition, Sony did not provide users with a convenient download site such as Apple's iTunes, which worked seamlessly with personal computers. Instead, it offered download services with limited selection, because other music companies refused to add their offerings to Sony Music's site. A complicated user interface turned consumers away especially because of its own strong copyright protection software, which restricted the number of downloads.[21] Sony's in-house music business created negative synergies instead of positive ones. Sony saw Apple's iPod and unknown companies such as iRiver or Rio destroying its business and capturing the digital music player market.[22]

Sony's performance in developing new digital music players is another example of both the legacy problem and the NIH (not-invented-here) syndrome. Sony had been so successful with CDs that it believed the market would immediately accept anything it offered. It believed that MD (MiniDisc) would succeed CD, and showed no interest in alternative products such as MP3 players. Even when MP3 players were introduced and sold well and became the de facto industry standard, Sony responded by introducing an upgraded version of MD, called the High MD, based on its own proprietary ATRAC format.

When iPods were released in Japan, Apple posted a slogan on commuter trains, "Goodbye MD," pointedly showing how Apple had nullified Sony's strategy. According to Christensen, incumbent market leaders are insensitive to "disruptive technological innovations," which are often inferior to existing technologies when they are introduced. For this reason, companies that introduce them look to new customers for growth, rather than targeting existing consumers. As the performance of disruptive new products improves and eventually exceeds that of old products, however, incumbent market leaders are replaced by these new entrants.

When trying to explain Sony's slow response to digital audio players, however, talking about legacy problem leaves many unanswered questions. Why did two of Sony's divisions introduce independently competing products? Why did Sony, which owns a vast array of music content," fail to create a wholly-owned product and service that was superior to Apple's iPod and iTunes? With the support and cooperation of its music and hardware sectors, it might have been possible to formulate a solution similar to iPod and iTunes that addressed the illegal file sharing issue. But Sony's global organizational structure obstructed such cooperation. And political power struggles among top executives of Sony's businesses further hindered cooperation.[23]

### The Heterogeneous PlayStation Business

PlayStation, Sony's game console, is the firm's biggest best seller since the Walkman and has been immensely profitable. Sony ventured into this business in 1991, after Nintendo broke up a joint development effort for a game platform that used CD-ROMs. The PlayStation synthesized the know-how Sony had accumulated in various computer-related businesses, and Sony has continued to encapsulate this know-how in its subsequent releases of PlayStation 2 and 3 and PSX.

The PlayStation business differed greatly from Sony's other businesses in terms of its organization and strategies. First, the PlayStation relied heavily on computers and software, and the business has been managed separately from Sony's other businesses. This separation has kept it insulated from Sony's analog culture, which vigorously opposed the inception of the PlayStation business and just about killed it before it was folded into Sony's Japanese music subsidiary. Even after PlayStation launched in 1994, says Kutaragi, an inventor of PlayStation, "many in Sony looked down on us because we were in games."[24] In fact, it took a long time for the digital concept to be accepted among Sony's engineers. Kutaragi described a hierarchy of Sony's engineers: "The top level was made up of analog circuit engineers, followed by mechanical engineers and structural engineers in charge of packaging and design. Digital engineers were at the bottom."[25] This observation concurs with a comment made by Sony's new CEO, Stringer: "We did not bring software engineers into the product development at the beginning. The engineers would begin the product and then software would come after the fact. And, that's because in a company that has jobs for life, the older people are at the top and the younger software engineers, of which there are many, are on the bottom, pushing up. So, there is a kind of a generation gap."[26]

For Sony, the PlayStation business is also different in that it has vertically integrated into semiconductor chips, which contrasts with

Idei's decision not to invest in flat panel displays. For PlayStation 2, Sony invested 250 billion yen to produce its own chips, and thereby capture more value.[27] For PlayStation 3, Sony invested 500 billion yen in production facilities for Cell, a next-generation microprocessor that Sony developed jointly with IBM and Toshiba for PS3 and Sony's other home electronics products. Kutaragi, who became the Corporate Vice President in 2003, tried to force the consumer electronics divisions to use Cell in their products, which incited fierce resistance. He had a vision that Sony should become an Intel in consumer electronics by supplying Cell for external demand and establishing it as the de facto standard, and he pushed for further internalization of parts and components that Sony relied on from external sources.[28] Kutaragi's strategy clearly countered that of Idei, who tried to create new services through network. Sony's top management team suffered from managerial schizophrenia.

Third, the initial product concept of the PlayStation was a game platform equipped with a CD player, but as the machine evolved to converge with Sony's other consumer electronics in terms of functionality, it increased the possibility of cannibalization. For example, when PlayStation 2 was released, Sony wanted this product to become the connecting path between home networks and broadband networks, so that users could watch DVD movies and listen to audio CDs with the DVD drive installed in PlayStation, play games, and also download various services by connecting the device to the Internet. As PlayStation evolves, it is thus highly probable that the PlayStation business will conflict with the video business.[29]

## Samsung Electronics' Digital Sashimi Shop

### Daring Investment, High-Speed Battle
Because the products it sells become commoditized so quickly, Samsung Electronics' strategic response to digital technology has been speed. Samsung Electronics has always been alert to the risk of entering these markets late, and a sense of crisis pervades the organization. In his video addresses, Yun constantly warns employees not to relax; he subscribes to the maxim of Intel's former CEO Andy Grove: "Only the paranoid survive."

Samsung Electronics' obsession over speed in digital products began when it started producing DRAM, for which prices drop very quickly (see Figure 2.3). The memory business is indeed "a battle with time" because a company can enjoy high price premiums only for a brief period until another competitor catches up. Samsung Electronics not only put a great deal of effort into learning how to produce DRAM but also completed its first production facility in six months, rather than the industry norm of two to three years. Samsung managers managed the plan, design, and construction of the facility—all at the same time. Samsung's managers and engineers stayed in barracks during the construction period, returning to their homes only once a week to change their clothes. When it began its initiative in DRAM technology, Samsung Electronics was about five years behind its Japanese competitors; the early completion of its first facility narrowed this gap by two years.

After it began making DRAM, Samsung Electronics then caught up with its competitors by aggressively expanding its production lines. It constructed a second line that produced 6-inch diameter wafers, a size that even technologically advanced competitors such as Intel and NEC deployed only for pilot lines. Samsung's engineers worked around the clock to improve efficiency in this new plant. Samsung Electronics repeated the same formulae with 8-inch wafers in the early 1990s, and 12-inch wafers in the late 1990s. As wafer sizes increased, the number of semiconductors out of a wafer was squared, but the manufacturing process became more complicated; it was more difficult to secure the same yield rate for chips and maintain consistent quality. And so Samsung Electronics' employees worked around the clock to increase yield and quality. Through their efforts, Samsung leapt ahead of its Japanese competitors.

Starting in the mid-1990s, Samsung Electronics then applied its magic formula—"Aggressive Investment and Speed"—to the TFT-LCD business. Initially, Samsung Electronics had defect rates as high as 40–50% on its 11-inch line for PCs. In the meantime, Japanese companies aggressively lowered their prices on these products. To respond, Samsung Electronics poured the cash it had earned from memory semiconductors into LCDs and then outflanked Japanese firms by starting a 12-inch line when Japanese competitors were still producing 11-inch models. Because of its aggressive investment,

Samsung Electronics reaped a profit of 1 trillion won in 1999. It then repeated this strategy to begin mass producing 17-inch, 32-inch, and 46-inch panels, just as it did in memory. The price of LCD screens has dropped by 30% annually (Figure 3.4), and the size of screens that consumers have wanted has continued to increase; so Samsung had to respond rapidly in order to survive. For instance, if consumer electronics firms typically released one product in a year, Samsung felt that it had to release two.

Similarly, Samsung Electronics' mobile phone business has thrived because its design engineers can complete the design for a new product within three to six months, and develop eight to ten new platforms per quarter. In contrast, Nokia and Motorola release only four to five new platforms a year, with a design cycle of 12 to 18 months. Samsung's

*Figure 3.4*   Price Drops in LCD TV (Worldwide Average Price)

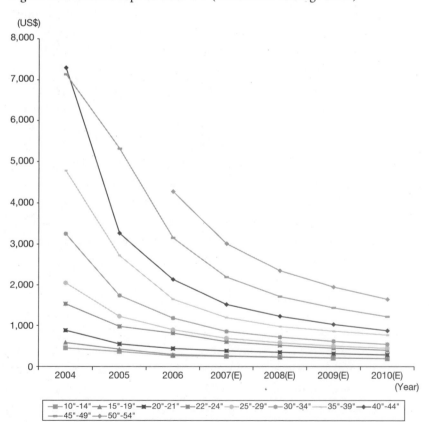

*Source:* Quarterly Global TV Shipment and Forecast Report, DisplaySearch, 2007.

mobile telecommunication division typically provides guidelines that define some parameters of a new product, and many development teams competitively design models on this basis; the competition among models speeds up new product development.

### Vertical Integration

Another competitive advantage of Samsung Electronics is its vertically integrated production process for key parts such as semiconductor or LCDs to end products. Samsung Electronics has attempted to control the "4Cs"—components such as semiconductors or LCDs, computers, communication, and consumer electronics in order to respond to two important trends of the digital age, convergence and broadband. Such control implies vertical integration,[30] which enhances the competitiveness of end products that use the components in which Samsung Electronics has its strength. For instance, the DRAM, flash memory, mobile phone chips, and ASICs that Samsung Electronics' semiconductor business has produced have gone to the firm's white goods appliances, computer, digital home appliance, communication, and living home appliance divisions. The LCD Division and Samsung SDI produce LCDs and PDP panels, respectively, and supply them to the TV business. There are still more subsidiaries that specialize in parts, such as Samsung Corning and Samsung Electro-mechanics, which supply parts to Samsung Electronics.

The vertically integrated business structure lowers procurement costs and enhances the speed of design, development, and production. The component businesses cooperate closely with businesses in end products, thus reinforcing Samsung Electronics' competitiveness in the latter part of the value chain. The component businesses supply parts to external customers and they try to maximize their own profits as separate business units. Still, because they are all Samsung subsidiaries, they are sensitive to other subsidiaries' needs.

Samsung Electronics not only purchases parts more cheaply through its affiliated suppliers but also uses supply chain management (SCM) to achieve fast delivery and low inventory. SCM paid off handsomely with its Bordeaux TV, which elevated Samsung Electronics to the world's number one position in the LCD TV segment in 2006. Samsung Electronics could supply products within two to four weeks of receiving an order from a foreign dealer. Such short delivery schedules are possible only with the timely supply of various raw materials. The SCM system precisely forecasts demands and globally optimizes the results in connection with enterprise resource planning (ERP) by considering variations in market demand, trends, past experience, and target market share. When demand falls, the system can quickly reduce supplies and stocks. Samsung Electronics often has its parts suppliers locate near its divisions to expedite research and development efforts that Samsung Electronics cannot handle with its internal resources.

### Lack of Creativity and Originality in New Product Development

Not all of Samsung Electronics' businesses are successful. Samsung Electronics focuses mainly on commodities, and excels only in technologies such as LCDs and mobile phones for which there are industry standards with clear trajectories. In businesses that require creative design or good software, or in businesses that lack clear technological road maps, the performance of Samsung Electronics has been much weaker.

For example, in customized or nonmemory semiconductors such as microprocessors, there is no clear trajectory. Instead, firms need to understand customer characteristics in order to develop products that incorporate new ideas. Nonmemory products require a long-term investment. The process of consultation, design, production, and sales takes over a year, and entails the risk that research and development will be wasted if the customer stops product development because of market fluctuations. Therefore, nonmemory products require strategic vision, long-term trust, creative engineers, and a liberal corporate culture. In the nonmemory business, "Each product has its own dynamics. For instance, fast product development is a key in mobile telecommunication. With PDA devices, it is critical to put multiple functions into one chip. Since each product requires somewhat different core competencies, Samsung cannot do well in everything. In addition, customers tend to take more initiative in product development and production. Samsung cannot develop simple and consistent strategies on its own, as it has done in the memory business. Samsung has been falling behind its competitors in understanding customers' demand for applications and in system integration skills."[31]

Even in 2006, Samsung Electronics' semiconductor business derives the great majority of its business from memory semiconductors.

To resolve this imbalance, and to insure itself against crashes in memory prices, Samsung Electronics has worked hard to build its nonmemory business. It has developed chipsets for HDTV (High Definition TV), DVD (Digital Video Disk), and CDMA (Code Division Multiple Access) communications chipsets. It has also sought to acquire technologies from foreign firms. In 1997, Samsung acquired the hardware division of 3DO, the U.S. game company, for $20 million. 3DO possessed technology for three-dimensional graphics, which Samsung executives believed the company could apply in other arenas of consumer electronics. Samsung dispatched 20 Korean engineers to the acquired business unit to transfer skills. It has also made several other equity investments in U.S.-based firms for the codevelopment of technology. For instance, it invested in CommQuest to develop mobile communications technology. Overall, however, Samsung executives have been disappointed with the results of these acquisitions.[32]

Perhaps Samsung Electronics' biggest weakness in the nonmemory businesses has been its approach. It has viewed these markets as being like the memory business, where a firm can succeed by investing heavily and waiting for the right opportunity. "The memory business requires a huge investment, but the payoff is also quick. One can recoup all the investment in just one year if there is an industry-wide shortage of chips. In contrast, it is hard to see results in the nonmemory business in a short period of time. You have to be willing to take losses for at least three to four years. If you are in a position to allocate resources between memory and nonmemory business, are you going to tell others that you want to invest in nonmemory business and take losses for three years? It is hard to do it since you know that you can recoup all your investment if you invest the same money in the memory business."[33]

*BusinessWeek* had an even more dire view of the problem: "DRAM makers have been like drug addicts saying they're going to quit. As soon as the market booms, they build more plants. They're addicted to the enormously high incremental profits."[34] To be successful in the nonmemory business, a firm has to develop long-term relations with customers based on trust, creative engineering, and a flexible corporate culture. "Logic chips are radically more complex than making DRAMs and usually require a nimble approach to design and marketing. Samsung's chip-manufacturing skills were first-rate, but the challenge would be to reform a rigid, hierarchical organization better suited

to producing commodities than logic chips."[35] Samsung Electronics'
corporate culture—its basis of success in the memory business—has
been a potential liability in nonmemory businesses.

Therefore, Samsung Electronics is focusing on nonmemory chips
that can be mass-produced, have big market potential, and show a
clear development trajectory. In other words, Samsung is looking for
nonmemory businesses that are most like the markets for memory chips.
DDI (Display Driver IC) and mobile chips are two main examples. It
is also endeavoring to develop integrated chips, for which it can utilize
its advantages in memory, such as combination chips that integrate
various functions, including memory, in one chip.

Samsung Electronics is also rather weak in consumer electronics,
except for LCD TVs, LCD computer monitors, and mobile phones.
It produces digital camcorders and digital cameras, but lacks basic
optical technologies, and has difficulty in sourcing them domestically.
Its PC and notebook divisions are focusing on domestic demand and
are falling behind competitors. Nor is its home appliance division,
which makes refrigerators and air conditioners, meeting consumers'
preferences. Rapid product development and cost savings, the sources
of Samsung's competitive advantage, are harder to apply in these areas.
For instance, although Samsung Electronics developed MP3 players
in 1999, its efforts in this market failed. It did not present designs
and advertisements that appealed to youth. Its managers did not pay
much attention to MP3 players because the market was originally far
smaller than its memory businesses were. Also, Samsung Electronics
was weak in software, such as DRM (Digital Rights Management) and
user interfaces, which made it difficult to produce a simple MP3 player.
In contrast, Apple's iPod had an innovative yet simple user interface,
and it knew exactly what younger generations' preferences were and
responded to them rapidly.

Samsung is not competitive in products for which creativity and
software matter and to which Samsung's magic formula, "speed and
aggressive investment," do not apply. So far, Samsung's strategy has
worked well when it was a follower. Unlike Sony, however, Samsung,
now a market leader itself, lacks the ability to develop new technology
and products when there is no clear trajectory or another firm for it
to benchmark. Furthermore, the foreign-trained Korean scientists and
engineers that Samsung relied on to absorb necessary technologies are

in short supply. And so Samsung Electronics has begun to accumulate technological know-how aggressively. It concentrated its group-level engineering staff, and established the Samsung Advanced Institute of Technology to develop basic science technologies that require long-term research and to develop cutting edge products. The institute includes several research divisions, including electronic devices, information systems, material parts, semiconductor communication, aerospace, and chemistry, which focuses on developing mid-term cutting edge technologies, and a basic technology sector. Furthermore, Samsung Electronics operates individual R&D organizations under each business division. There, once the basic concept of the new product is set, the R&D organizations within business divisions initiate research on design. Competition among research organizations is inevitable. For example, the Digital Media Division, which makes PDAs (Personal Digital Assistant), and the Telecommunication Network Division have developed competing products in the past. To prevent such overlaps and to decrease this competition, Samsung Electronics created a CTO (Chief Technology Officer) function in 2004. This office manages mid- to long-term basic research, road mapping and patent standardization, and integrates/controls the R&D functions of each general department. It also drafts personnel when an R&D project team is organized. In addition, Samsung Electronics built a new Digital Research Center building in 2006 to enhance cooperation among its research organizations. This building houses more than 5,000 researchers from throughout the company. This colocation will facilitate information sharing and product development, and will reduce costs.

Nonetheless, Samsung Electronics' disappointing results in its overseas acquisitions suggest areas for improvement. Unless it can improve the performance of these investments, or acquire further globalization capabilities to utilize foreign employees' technological skills, the company will face difficulty in developing new technologies and products in the future.

### Apple's iPod

Early in the twenty-first century, a new trend emerged in the music market. Consumers stopped purchasing packaged music on CDs and replaying songs with a separate CD player and instead began storing only the songs they liked on their own computers and sharing these files with their friends. Steve Jobs, Apple Computer's CEO, found out that many Mac users downloaded MP3 files from online sharing sites, listened to this music on their home and work computers and on portable CD players by burning the files into CDs. At the time, Mac products contained neither CD burners, nor programs that could manage thousands of MP3 files. Jobs made Apple's engineers install CD-ROM burners as basic options in all Mac products. To get the right software, Jobs purchased a company called SoundStep, established by Jeff Robbin. Within several months, Robbin presented the first iTunes program, and Jobs demonstrated iTunes to the public in 2001 at the MacWorld Trade Show. The response was amazing. People loved the simple and easy-to-use interface and the technology that enabled the users to conveniently classify and manage thousands of songs.[36]

Jobs already sensed the advent of a revolution in the music market. He concluded that this revolution would not be complete unless a new portable device to replace the CD player was released, and he encouraged Robbin to develop programs for portable devices. In November 2001, the iPod prototype was released. To free users from the inconvenience of buying CDs and extracting music files into MP3 formats, and to let them obtain good MP3 files online, Jobs also decided to open an online music store.

Yet Jobs also needed a powerful copyright protection program to satisfy the concerns of music content firms, and he needed to convince these firms to sell their music online through iTunes. At the time, the music market was trapped in a recession because illegal file sharing was rampant through P2P (peer-to-peer) download sites such as Kazaa or Napster. The major music labels were struggling to find a business model that could protect their copyrights and generate revenue through the online music market. Although there were already two major online music sites operated by alliances of large producers, that is, Pressplay by Universal and Sony, and Music Net by AOL Time Warner, Bertelsmann, EMI, and Realnetworks, these sites were incompatible and failed to satisfy users' diverse demands. The music labels had secured only a small number of users through their online music stores, and were watching helplessly as free file-sharing sites destroyed their market. In 2002, BMG laid off 1,400 employees, Sony 1,000, and EMI 1,800. This result was inevitable. Their operating margin had shrunk from 15% to 5%.

When Jobs entered the online music market, music companies and PC manufacturers distrusted one another; the music companies believed that PC manufacturers condoned the distribution of illegal MP3 files, in order to increase their PC sales. As the CEO of Pixar, a digital animation studio that had released several hit films, Jobs was in a position to understand the needs of both content and hardware businesses. He asked the major labels (Universal, EMI, Sony, BMG, Warner) to discard their access fee-based business model, and he asserted that consumers should own the files they downloaded. Of course, most of the music labels were very doubtful about his ideas, but Jobs secured a contract for one year. The business model let Apple take 33% of the sales, which was 99 cents per song, and give the balance of 66 cents to the music labels.

Apple's online music site, iTunes Music Store, allowed consumers to burn CDs and share the files they downloaded with others by storing them in their iPods. iTunes could synchronize music files between PCs and the iPod automatically, once the iPod was connected to the PC, as well as automatically charge the iPod. There was a function that automatically classified the songs into categories, and a shuffling function to select and listen to favored songs only. Apple's unique music file format, AAC, was qualitatively better than MP3, and Apple was enthusiastically supported by the users, who could now buy individual songs instead of paying $20 for a CD that contained many songs they didn't want. Moreover, Apple encrypted all the files, making them playable on only three authorized computers. By doing so, Apple was able to obstruct the possibility of sharing files through systems such as Kazaa. By 2006, Apple had sold over 1 billion songs through iTunes Music Store, and by April 2007, five years after the first iPod was released, it had sold 100 million iPods. In contrast, Sony's Walkman took 13 years to sell 100 million units. "iPod was one of the biggest hits ever."[37]

Unlike Sony, Apple did not have any core capabilities in the audio sector. It produced iPod by combining its core capabilities in computer OS and software with an innovative product design developed by a start-up company it acquired. Sony, however, had made many missteps that prevented it from capturing the MP3 market, despite possessing most of the assets required to succeed.

# 4

# New Kids on the Block

We must produce things that can appeal people's hearts. This means that they should be good-looking and with great functionality, and make those people who use them happy. If a company keeps releasing products that consumers want, its brand image will naturally improve.

*—Norio Ohga, former CEO of Sony*[1]

Samsung is the poster child for using design to increase brand value and market share.

*—Patrick Whitney, Director of the Institute of Design at the Illinois Institute of Technology*[2]

Sony has been perceived as a synonym for "smart and unique products, good performance, and outstanding design." People are so familiar with Sony that some Western consumers never realize that Sony is a Japanese company. As a global brand, Sony is ranked as highly as Coca-Cola or Nike. In comparison, Samsung was a completely generic brand until the mid-1990s. Its products sat unnoticed at the bottom of store shelves. Consumers perceived them as cheap.

This gap in perceptions has narrowed considerably. In a brand value assessment, conducted by Interbrand in 2000, the brand values of Samsung and Sony were ranked 43rd and 18th, respectively. By 2006, Samsung had moved to 20th, and Sony had dropped to 26th (see Figure 4.1).[3] This shift occurred because Samsung Electronics had fully capitalized on the opportunities made possible by the digital revolution in marketing and technology. Because there are no noticeable differences in quality among digital products that share the same features, it is easier for latecomers to catch up with market leaders. Samsung Electronics thus caught up with Japanese consumer electronics companies. However, other latecomers, such as Chinese companies, may catch up with Samsung Electronics. Therefore, in the digital age, brand and marketing strategies are even more important than they were in the analog age.

*Figure 4.1*   Brand Values, Rankings, and Advertising Expenses of Sony and Samsung Electronics

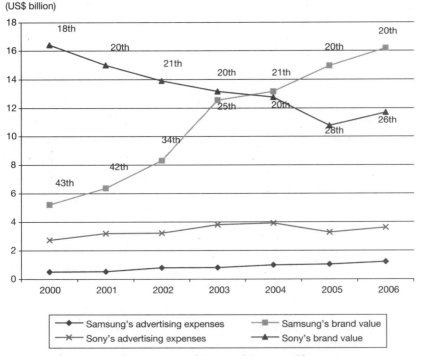

*Source:* Interbrand, Auditing Report of Sony and Samsung Electronics.

To reinforce its brand value, Samsung Electronics has concentrated many of its resources in the mobile phone business, its flagship area, and strategically promoted specialized distribution channels for consumer electronics. In contrast, Sony's marketing strategy, which has revolved around new product development stopped working when Sony was no longer able to release new, unique products. Also, Sony is under great pressure from distributors, which have gained negotiating power over manufacturers, especially since digital products have become mainstream.

## Sony's Marketing Strategy: Focusing on New Products

### New Product Development and Brand

Sony understood the importance of brand from its inception. The origin of "Sony" shows the global mindset of its founders; who coined the brand name Sony in 1955 because it was easier for Western consumers to pronounce. "Sony" sounded cute, like the pet name Sonny, but it also meant *sonus*, or "sound," in Latin. In 1958, the firm adopted this brand name as its corporate name.

When Morita went to the United States with a Sony-branded radio in 1955, a major manufacturer suggested: "the price is right, we will order 100,000 units. But under one condition; these won't sell in the name Sony. Let's label them with our brand. No one knows who Sony is in America."[4] At that time, an order of this size was very attractive to Sony. Yet Morita turned the offer down and insisted on maintaining the brand name. With this episode etched in his memory, he returned to Japan firmly resolved to grow Sony into a world-class brand. Sony has managed its brand assiduously since then. For example, when opening Sony shops, Sony even regulates the font sizes of the signboards and the layout of the products to suit the brand image. In TV advertisements, Sony has consistently emphasized its corporate image by inserting the line "It's a Sony." Ohga, Sony's former CEO, also changed the Sony logo several times before the most recent version was officially adopted in 1973.

The essence of Sony's marketing strategy was to develop new products that consumers truly craved. According to Morita, Sony focused on new products development because its bigger competitors were always right behind, imitating its products. If Sony failed to come up with new products, competitors could overtake it. Morita said that their plan was "to lead the public with new products rather than ask them what kind of products they want. The public does not know what is possible, but we do. So, instead of doing a lot of market research, we refine our thinking on a product and its use and try to create a market for it by educating and communicating with the public."[5] The Walkman was a case in point. When Morita ordered Sony's engineers to remove the recording circuit and speaker to make a light-weight portable player, upon hearing Ibuka's complaint after a long business trip, many of Sony's employees doubted whether any consumer would ever want such a product. Morita said, "I do not believe that any amount of market research could have told us that the Sony Walkman would be successful, not to say a sensational hit that would spawn many imitators."[6]

Sony's marketing strategies typically conveyed the concepts of its new products to consumers. In 1975, when Sony released the Betamax VCR, its marketing plan advertised the idea of a "time shift" to make consumers realize that they could record TV programs they liked, but had to miss, and then watch them later. Morita said, "It was my idea that we had to create a market for the video cassette recorder by educating people and giving them new ideas. I gave speeches telling people Betamax was really something new. 'Now you can grab a TV program in your hand,' I said. 'With the VCR, television is like a magazine—you can control your own schedule.' This is the concept I wanted to sell. I knew that the competition would soon be upon us, and I wanted to beat it and move people into VCR as fast as possible."[7]

With the advent of the digital age, Sony, the analog king, had premonitions of doom. Idei warned his employees, "the 40 and over generations still buy products by brand, but brand loyalty is becoming weaker daily among the younger generation. It's hard to give the digital product a special character or uniqueness. Still, however, we'll fall behind if we just idle around, not making something new, something unique that only Sony can make."[8] Sony's CTO (Chief Technology Officer) also emphasized craftsmanship, saying that "in the digital age, it's hard to make a differentiated product, and therefore that should be the new challenge for Sony to overcome."[9]

Sony's brand has grown weaker because it has not introduced any unique products since it brought out PlayStation in the mid-1990s. As the value of the Sony name has faded, consumers have become less willing to pay a premium for the brand. Also, because Sony's brand value resulted from a constant release of new products instead of intentional promotion, Sony lacked clear marketing strategies for enhancing brand value, and thus had no measures to prevent its brand value from deteriorating once the new product pipeline dried up.

## Product Design and Advertisement

Sony has supported its new products with fashionable product designs and advertisements. When Ohga joined Sony in 1959, there was no consistency in how products were conceived, designed, or advertised.[10] Advertising was done by another sales subsidiary. Designers for each product were assigned separately to their respective planning departments, and there was no cooperation among them. In the 1960s, as other big Japanese electronics firms entered the radio market and Sony's market share dropped, Morita asked Ohga to take charge of product planning.

Ohga believed that in order to make an attractive product, clear "product development" and "industrial design" were necessary. He initiated the design idea of "black and silver," which harmonized the silver tone of metal and black of plastic. Ohga also thought that consistency in design would help Sony set forth a coherent image. He established the principle that product planning should be integrated with design and advertising, and he unified design into a Design Division, which had been previously scattered in various product development departments. He also established the Creative Center, which coordinated overall design. In addition, Oga asserted that there should be advanced planning for advertisements and promotion catchphrases.

PlayStation has been the most successful electronic product in history. Its success was greatly indebted to its design, which was a combination of circles and squares. The controllers were made in horn shapes instead of the traditional flat shape. Teiyu Goto, who later designed VAIO, was the designer. Sony's VAIO computer was not much different from other PCs when it was first introduced, but in 1997, Sony released a light-weight, thin, strong notebook PC made of magnesium compound. It added a touch of purple, a novel color for a notebook PC in those days, and achieved great success in the PC business. Sony advertised VAIO by saying that it was highly compatible with AV devices, and that consumers could send video clips taken with its video cameras through e-mails with VAIO. Likewise, Sony's advertisements centered on newly released products. Under this principle, the release date of PlayStation was set for more effective advertising copy. For instance, before the release of PlayStation 3, Sony used a teaser ad, which said "1, 2, 3, don't miss December [12] 3rd PlayStation will change the game world."[11] Such tactics helped Sony maintain its high price premium.

**Distribution and Price Policies**

Sony surpassed other firms in building a powerful brand and securing product development capacities, but it paid less attention to distribution channels and price policies. It seemed that Sony approached distribution channels with the assumption that anything it made would succeed, because all its products were "one-and-only," and all the distributors had to do was to pass along its products to consumers.

Morita seemed to regard distribution channels as a necessary evil. He once said, "In the traditional Japanese system for distributing consumer products, the manufacturers are kept at arm's length from the consumer. Communication is all but impossible. There are primary, secondary, and even tertiary wholesalers dealing with some goods before they reach a retailer and the ultimate user of the product. This distribution system has some social value—it provides plenty of jobs—but it is costly and inefficient."[12] This casts light on Morita's revolt against the traditionally complicated distribution structure in Japan. He continued, "We realized from the beginning that it could not serve the needs of our company and its new, advanced technology products. Third or fourth parties simply could not have the same interest in or enthusiasm for our products and our ideas that we had. We had to educate our customers to the uses of our products. To do so, we had to set up our own outlets and establish our own ways of getting goods into the market."[13]

Because consumers came into stores specifically to look for Sony products, Sony saw no reason to give the dealers high margins to have them encourage consumers to purchase its products. Sony also did not use strategic marketing and failed to allocate marketing resources for key strategic markets or products. It did not consider how to market its products in some important overseas markets. Although it recognized the importance of major emerging markets such as Brazil, Russia, India, and China in early 2000, and formulated strategies to actively penetrate them, it did not sufficiently invest in and support these strategies. Sony did not increase its budget for advertising in these markets either.

Sony wanted to bypass middlemen such as dealers or wholesalers, if possible, and directly communicate with end users. Take a look at its release of PlayStation in 1994. Nintendo, which ruled the game industry prior to Sony's entry, manufactured the game software in Mask ROMs. Mask ROMs can access data more quickly, but involve a long manufacturing process that makes reproduction difficult. And so it took months to reorder popular games. Therefore, game manufacturers, afraid of losing sales opportunities, tried to produce many copies of their games when they first produced them. Then, if these games did not sell, wholesalers had too many unpopular games in stock. In addition, much-used software was sold as if it was new.

Sony adopted the CD-ROM system to fundamentally reform the distribution system. For software developers, Sony's strategy was way more profitable, since the CD-ROMs cost only one-quarter to one-third of Nintendo's Mask ROM formats, and could be reproduced in just a couple of days. There was no risk of accumulating stock. Further, the cheap prices induced consumers to buy more new software. Software writers were enthusiastic about the CD-ROM format, even if they had to pay the same royalty to Sony. Consequently, Sony destroyed the wholesaler-centered distribution channel Nintendo had previously built, thus bringing about a system in which it directly provided software titles to retailers.[14]

## The Marketing Strategy of the Latecomer, Samsung Electronics

### Marketing Strategy in Transition
Until the early 1990s, everyone thought of Samsung as a cheap, generic brand. The perception was especially strong in the U.S. market, which Samsung had entered early when its products were of poor quality, and

somewhat less so in the European market, which it entered later. Until the late 1990s, Sony's VCRs were sold for almost double the price that Samsung's were, even when both had similar functionality; the price gap was attributable mainly to their brands. It was only in 1994, when Chairman Kun-hee Lee initiated the "New Management Movement," to emphasize quality over quantity, that Samsung Electronics began realizing the importance of brands. Lee initiated this movement after he visited U.S. stores and saw how serious Samsung's brand problem was. Samsung Electronics began to conduct activities to promote its brand, such as launching *Je-kap-bap-ki*, which means "receiving the full value of a product," increasing its price, and improving quality while sacrificing sales.

In 1997, Samsung Electronics conducted an internal study that found when market conditions change due to digitalization, Samsung Electronics would completely founder within a few years if it maintained its current product portfolio. This spread the fever for change throughout the firm. Digital technology not only made it possible for Samsung Electronics to catch up with other consumer electronics firms, but also for firms with cheaper labor costs to catch up to Samsung. Without a strong brand, how could anyone survive in the future?

### Advertising and Brand Strategies

In 1995, under the leadership of the former CEO Kwang-ho Kim, Samsung Electronics set aside a marketing fund of US$400 million for investment in 10 emerging markets to elevate its brand. Because it had traditionally pursued strategies of expanding market share by cutting costs and using economies of scale, Samsung Electronics had been dominated by engineers and financial controllers, and its marketing personnel had been third-class citizens. Senior management now decided that it was necessary to bring in an outsider, preferably a foreigner, to head the marketing function, because it was not easy to convince managers to spend money on marketing. Eric Kim, a Korean-American, who became Samsung Electronics' director of global marketing in 1999, described the idea of marketing within the firm: "Our managers believed that good products sell themselves, and that marketing was nothing more than selling, and that selling was only needed when you had a me-too or weak product. I had worked hard for four years to educate our divisional managers on the role of marketing and the value of developing and communicating superior solutions for our target customers. We have made progress, but many Samsung managers responded initially with a 'show me' attitude."[15] Samsung Electronics' CEO voiced strong support for Kim, when introducing him to other executives, "Anyone trying to shake this guy up is going to get in trouble."

Samsung Electronics realized that it was necessary to instill a marketing orientation throughout the company. The firm conducted various forms of education and training, while organizing teams and divisions to manage marketing systematically. It created a marketing team within the Overseas Business HQ in 1995, which took charge of regional strategies, product strategies, and overseas projects. In 1999, it organized a company-wide "Global Marketing Team," including a Brand Strategy Team, Product Innovation Team, and Regional Strategy Team.

Samsung Electronics' Global Marketing Team set up a brand mission and a credo to create consensus among employees, and it taught production workers and managers that a brand is something like a promise to the customers. It taught that a brand is not a mere advertisement, but an important asset to be protected and invested in. To develop internal consensus, the team tried to quantify the firm's brand value in order to justify its investment in the brand and avoid internal opposition from Samsung Electronics' finance-oriented corporate culture. With the help of a consulting company, the team calculated Samsung Electronics' brand value in 2000 as being around $5.2 billion. After Samsung Electronics spent $508 million for advertising in 2000, the estimate of Samsung Electronics' brand value increased to $6.3 billion in 2001 (See Figure 4.1). Of course, even the marketing team realized that there were many problems in quantifying brand value, and no one could be sure of a linkage between marketing expenses in one year to the overall brand value. Nevertheless, the Global Marketing Team used this increase to claim that the advertising expense for that year had a rate of return on investment of over 200% and to justify continuous future investment in the brand.

Even so, it required much more investment for the Samsung brand to be finally acknowledged as a high-quality, high-end product by overseas consumers. Until 1993, Samsung Electronics had spent about 1% of sales for advertising. From 1994 onward, it increased its advertising expenditures to over 2% of sales. The corporate office also required overseas subsidiaries to adopt a unified worldwide ad campaign, and made sure that those overseas subsidiaries spent at least 3.5% of their sales for advertisement, in order to prevent them from cutting down advertising expenses to increase their profits.

As for investment in individual products, Samsung Electronics concentrated most of its marketing resources in mobile phones after identifying them as having the highest ROI (return on investment) in advertising; after all, mobile phones have a high degree of brand exposure, and consumers carry their phones with them all the time. Also, Samsung Electronics' mobile phones were positioned as mostly high-end, multifunctional products that were new and cool. The enhanced image of Samsung mobile phones was very useful in improving Samsung's brand image overall. By concentrating the company's marketing resources on mobile phones, Samsung Electronics' mobile phone business attained third place in the industry, with a market share of 10.5% in 2003, up from a market share of 2.7% in 1998.

Samsung Electronics focused on emphasizing the "digital" aspect of its products. It ran an ad that said "Samsung digital, everyone is invited." The idea was to highlight an open, friendly, high-tech digital image. The core message was that consumers could enjoy a better, more exciting life if they used Samsung Electronics' easy-to-use digital devices for communication, entertainment, and information.

After this campaign, Samsung Electronics sponsored the film *Matrix Reloaded*, in which its high-tech mobile phones were prominently placed. Furthermore, Samsung Electronics used the Matrix motif in its ads for mobile phones, computer monitors, and digital camcorders. The headline of an ad in Figure 4.2, "Rotating Realities," invited consumers, familiar with the movie, to capture the realities with its rotating camera phone. Another message of this ad may have been to remind consumers of the true value of the emerging Samsung brand. Samsung Electronics also focused on sports marketing, which had the best effect on enhancing brand awareness. It sponsored the Olympics and other sports. It consolidated its advertising and actively implemented a branding strategy. Through these efforts, as noted above, the ranking of Samsung Electronics' brand went from 43rd in 2000 to 20th in 2006.

*Figure 4.2*   Samsung Electronics' Matrix Advertisement

Courtesy of Samsung Electronics and Warner Brothers.

## Distribution Channels and Pricing Strategies

Samsung Electronics also began focusing on certain markets and restructuring its distribution channels in the mid-1990s. It selected 10 "emerging markets" and allocated strategic marketing budgets for each one, such as special budgets for extra advertising and hiring local marketing specialists, which contrasted with Sony's inability to mobilize into emerging markets. Also, starting in 1995, it began marketing designed to sell its products for prices that suited the products' actual quality, and starting monitoring the status of products' value versus their market prices.

For instance, in the North American market, Samsung Electronics' products had been used as loss leaders to attract cheap consumers at large discount stores such as Sears, Wal-Mart, and Kmart. In the mid-1990s, however, Samsung Electronics began to avoid the discount store sales channel, and attempted to sell only to a small number of specialty electronics stores such as Best Buy. Because it lacked brand equity, it had to act differently in order to sell its low-profile products. It therefore adopted a high price, a high-margin policy, and gave dealers incentives to sell its products.

Although not all of its initial efforts were successful, Samsung Electronics eventually gained a foothold in this segment. Circuit City, for instance, refused to sell Samsung Electronics' products until the late 1990s. In spring 1998, after Samsung Electronics gave an hour-long presentation, a Circuit City manager nearly slammed the door in the presenters' face. "Please don't come back again," he said, "unless you have the only product in the world or the cheapest product in the world." After that incident, Samsung Electronics established a close relationship with Best Buy, and jointly promoted advertising and events. At one point, the proportion of Samsung Electronics' sales in the United States through Best Buy reached as high as 30%. As Samsung Electronics improved its market position, however, Circuit City approached Samsung and asked if Circuit City could sell its products.

Samsung Electronics also reorganized its sales regions. Instead of using sales representatives, it placed a direct sales force in major cities and regions such as New York, Washington, DC, Los Angeles, San Francisco, Chicago, Dallas, and Florida to manage these distribution channels. This reorganization of sales channels helped the firm increase its sales volume while repositioning its products as high-price and high-quality. In regard to marketing activities, the biggest difference between Samsung Electronics and Sony is that Samsung actively invested in strategically important markets and Sony concentrated only on its capacities to develop new products. Sony's high brand image may have resulted from brilliant new products, but Samsung earned its image through deliberate marketing efforts.

Samsung's earnest effort to concentrate its marketing resources to specialty distributors drastically contrasts with Sony's fragmented approach. According to an analyst at Goldman Sachs, "Sony has currently more than 4,000 sales forces to generate $10 billion sales in the U.S. Samsung does not need such a large sales force since it is targeting only a small number of national retailers. With the cost saving, Samsung can put more money in promotion and advertisement."

### New Product Development Strategy

Samsung Electronics redoubled its efforts to enhance product design strengths and develop innovative new products. Traditionally, its designers had a very minor role in modifying products' packaging or looks; the product development unit had already made such decisions. Moreover, in most cases, the firm's CEO or business division presidents personally selected product designs that they favored. In the past, Samsung Electronics' products were me-too items; they were imitations or late versions of products released by market leaders such as Sony. For example, by the time the New Management Movement was launched, Samsung's 29-inch or 32-inch TVs still had a cheap, low-quality, me-too image. Samsung was not able to manufacture projection TVs until the mid-1990s due to its lack of technological know-how. After it implemented this movement, Samsung attempted to develop a "power brand," such as the World's Best TVs. Because it was merely using technologies that were no better than those that others used, however, it could not command a premium. Further, consumers did not notice its efforts to add new functions and enhance quality, so Samsung Electronics could not offset its production costs by increasing the final product price.

Ever since he launched the New Management Movement, Chairman Lee has constantly emphasized the importance of design. For instance, he declared in 1996 that "design would be a source of corporate competitiveness in the new century." His group-level staff organization executed various measures to drive this competition. Samsung Group established IDS (Innovative Design Lab of Samsung) in 1996, and hired six foreign professors to teach design courses to designers from Samsung Group's various affiliates. As a result, its products, including mobile phones, DVDs, and TFT-LCDs, won the Industrial Design Excellence Award by the American Industrial Design Association in 2003. In 2004, Samsung Electronics became the top-ranked firm for design excellence.

Samsung Electronics also created a "strategic product system" to develop new products. This system institutes a tight time schedule. Employees generate ideas for product concepts from March to April, the business division presidents present the ideas in front of the CEO in May and June, and three items are chosen as the strategic products for the following year, meaning that HQ will support all marketing expenses after the release of these new products. According to this timetable, all business divisions work round-the-clock to develop new and better products. Samsung Electronics' Bordeaux LCD TV, released in early 2006, was developed through this strategic product system. It went through a thorough process reengineering of product planning, market research, design, marketing and distribution using the "VIP (Value Innovation Project) room" for three months.

The VIP Room is a facility that has lodgings, over 20 project rooms, conference rooms, and saunas, for team members on a specific project to concentrate on work.[16] Samsung's top engineers and designers are called into the VIP room to complete an important product development mission. Having a dormitory and a sauna on site means that its guests will stay there for a long time without going back home. The VIP Room is depicted as "an invitation-only round-the-clock assembly line for ideas."[17] Samsung Electronics attempted to arrange new product development, which requires creativity, as if it was a mass production process. "When people are told they have to come here, they know they have to come up with results in a very, very short time," says a veteran team leader.[18] "Samsung executives acknowledge—with obvious pride—that the building is occupied 24 hours a day, seven days a week. And even if they don't sleep over, 18- to 20-hour days are not uncommon."

Samsung Electronics decided to begin the VIP program because its management realized that about 80% of a product's cost and quality were determined in the initial stage of product development. The VIP team that made the Bordeaux TV began its work with the goal of developing a million-seller LCD TV. Eleven teammates spent three months together and released the product only after thoroughly researching the design, product specifications, release date, dealers' responses, and price premiums.

With everyone together in one place, it was easier to develop an innovative product than it would have been if designers, engineers, and product planners worked separately and focused only on product features that were relevant to their function.[19] The Bordeaux TV team used the method of value innovation.[20] It omitted functions that customers did not use, improved picture quality, and created a beautiful design in the shape of a wine glass because the designers realized that consumers thought of large TVs as being like expensive pieces of furniture. The finished product had fewer functions with buttons on the side. The rear side had the same finish as the front for purely aesthetic reasons.

Compared to Sony's efforts to develop new, innovative products, however, Samsung Electronics' Bordeaux TV is the outcome of a narrowly focused project, and is a conventional, albeit fancy, TV. The company did not expect that the team would come up with a radically new product in just three months. Its perspective is that creativity can be cultivated and reinforced by investment and training;[21] this belief firmly grounds the goal of new product development system in the idea of mass production. Even if researchers' creativity is viewed as important, having them complete product development according to a strict timetable is something only Samsung Electronics could imagine doing. Maybe the idea worked this time, but how many people can continue to be creative under constant time pressure?[22]

Samsung Electronics has recognized that it could use more creativity; Chairman Lee declared "creative management" was an important management agenda for 2007, and the firm has hired much creative talent from overseas. There are many foreigners in Samsung Electronics' six Design Centers, five of which are abroad, to make up for the limitations of Korean designers. In the past, engineers told designers to come up with a specific product, but designers are now telling the engineers what functions they want. The employees working at Design Centers increased to 450, a 50% increase, during 2002–2004, and the company is trying to supplement its creative workforce, its "S-level talent," by scouting talented candidates from the outside. A marketing specialist comments on this trend: "We no longer use the word 'benchmarking.' These days, we do cross-industry benchmarking, but don't do it anymore in the same industry. Even if we do, it's just for reference. In the past, we could benchmark competitors and quickly imitate them, but now there's no one to benchmark. Since there is no one to benchmark and since we know that we are not creative enough, the management is feeling uneasy about this."

## Increasing Bargaining Power of Retailers

### Consolidation of Distribution

Samsung Electronics has worked hard to prove that it is no longer a "low price, low quality, and therefore worthless brand." In contrast to Sony, which has concentrated only on the first of the four Ps in marketing, Product, Samsung has focused extensively on the other 3Ps, Price, Place (specialty electronics stores rather than discount chains), and Promotion. When Sony introduces a new product, for instance, it releases detailed promotional materials and videos that demonstrate how consumers can use it. It does not, however, pay much attention to distribution and pricing.

Nevertheless, the distribution sector has undergone substantial consolidation in the last decade. Large distributors such as Best Buy, Circuit City, and Yamaha Denki have emerged in the United States, Japan, and Europe. Distributors' massive volume, accessibility, and enormous bargaining power may affect the future profitability of Sony and Samsung Electronics. These distributors display the products of several companies at their stores, so consumers can compare these items easily. In the analog age, the quality of each product differed radically, and the brand itself had the most influence on consumers' choices. Now, because the quality of digital products is so similar, consumers often rely heavily on the advice given by store personnel and show greater loyalty to certain distributors than they do to manufacturers' brands. Frequent-buyer programs offered by distributors, such as point systems, bring consumers even closer to distributors and further from manufacturers. This trend demonstrates the shift in power from manufacturers to distributors that digital technology has brought about.

In Japan, where numerous consumer electronics manufacturers compete fiercely with each other in their small but dense home markets, electronics distributors are engaged in "focused merchandising," which involves reducing the number of manufacturers they deal

*Figure 4.3* Profitability of Electronics Manufacturers and Distributors in Japan

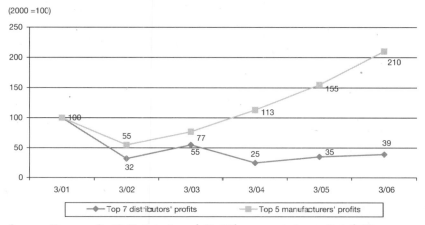

(2000 =100)

Top 7 distributors' profits
Top 5 manufacturers' profits

*Source:* Kawaso, S., Y. Fujimori, and K. Nihonyanagi. Japan Retail: Consumer Electronics Value Chain, Goldman Sachs, Cross-Sector Report, May 25, 2005.

with, as a way to pressure manufacturers. For example, the biggest Japanese consumer electronics distributor, Yamaha Denki, handles fewer manufacturers than its smaller competitors do. According to Goldman Sachs, Yamaha handles three LCD TV brands, Sharp, Sony, and Sanyo. Smaller distributors, such as Kojima or K's Denki, offer a much wider array of choices.[23] By dealing with a small number of consumer electronics manufacturers, large distributors lower their unit purchase price and receive various sorts of promotional support. If smaller distributors adopt focused merchandising in the future, distributors' negotiating power will be further enhanced, which may further threaten manufacturers' profitability. Figure 4.3 shows the profits of five Japanese consumer electronics manufacturers and seven consumer electronics distributors during 2000–2005. Distributors' profits increased consistently, while producers' became less than one-third of what they had been in 2000.

## The Responses of Sony and Samsung Electronics

Sony has long preferred selling its products through direct sales channels rather than going through conventional wholesalers/retailers. Idei believed that relying on existing distribution channels was outdated and unfit for the future network society, and so he began attempting to sell products online through a site called "Sony Style" in 2002. Sony also opened up Sony Style stores in the United States. The inspiration for this venture came from Dell's remarkable success in the PC business, a representative commodity product. Dell accepted online orders for customized production, ridding itself of distribution margins and inventory costs, and purchasing computer parts for the cheapest prices because the prices for parts are constantly decreasing. Sony believed that it could apply Dell's direct sales strategy to digital consumer electronics and thereby circumvent increasingly powerful distributors. Sony intended to start by selling VAIO computers and PDAs and gradually expanding to other products.

Sony's direct sales strategy has, however, faced serious conflict with existing distribution channels. Retailers that have long sold Sony products have attacked Sony Style, and even Sony's own sales department, tailored to conventional channels, is hostile toward Sony Style. Despite Idei's orders to support Sony Style, the sales department has inevitably been more sensitive toward the complaints of the distribution channels, with which they have had to deal personally. Sony Style has not grown as much as Sony initially projected.

Meanwhile, Samsung Electronics has reinforced its relationship with distribution channels in order to improve its negotiations with them, and is attempting to reap cost advantages and profit in components rather than end products. Because Samsung Electronics is producing key components internally for digital consumer electronics, such as DRAMs, flash memories, LCD panels, and mobile phone parts, it has very large cost advantages over its competitors. In short, thanks to its vertically integrated business structure and its cost competitiveness in the component business, Samsung Electronics enjoys constant profitability in the increasingly hard-to-differentiate field of digital electronics. Samsung Electronics' close relationship with large distributors is an additional plus.

## Samsung's New Management Movement

Chairman Kun-hee Lee of Samsung Group succeeded the firm's founder, the late Byung-chull Lee, who died in 1987. Ever since he became Chairman, he has emphasized change and reform, declaring a "second founding," and has attempted to instill a sense of urgency in Samsung's executives. Yet these managers showed no signs of changing for years. In 1993, Samsung Electronics hosted a technology development meeting in Japan. There, Japanese advisors hired by Chairman Lee frankly discussed their impressions of Samsung Electronics. Among them, an advisor named Shigeo Fukuda submitted a report about the technologies Samsung must procure and about various ways to improve the product development process, summarizing his opinion of Samsung. Chairman Lee, who then went to Frankfurt, received a videotape that showed how defective Samsung's assembly process for washing machines was. After his disappointment earlier that year, when he saw what American consumers thought of Samsung's products, Lee was enraged and ordered all of Samsung's executives to congregate in Frankfurt. The Frankfurt Conference, held on June 7, 1993, signaled the start of the New Management Movement. After this meeting, Lee visited Osaka, Tokyo, and London, to lecture executives and employees about the need for innovation.

Under the "Samsung New Management" slogan, Chairman Lee pursued "quality-centered management," "globalization," and "integration" as ways to reinforce the firm's competitiveness and become a world-class company in the twenty-first century. These goals were attempts to respond to fundamental changes, such as the increasing importance of software, globalization, and technological integration. Quality-centered management is an attempt to improve competitiveness by achieving quality improvements. It encompasses both products and people. Samsung Group considers it to be the precondition for globalization and integration.

Globalization is the stepping stone for Samsung to improve its overall management, including technology, quality, and marketing, and to catch up with other market leaders. Integration is about generating organic synergies from interrelated infrastructure, facilities, functions, technologies, and software, as well as maximizing competitiveness and efficiency. In short, the overall goal of the movement was to reinforce the idea that Samsung could create a huge synergetic effect and become a top-tier enterprise if it could concentrate and integrate its various strengths.

This movement got underway as executives summarized and detailed Chairman Lee's comments and organized task forces to execute new initiatives. Employees were supposed to believe that "I must be the one to change first in order to survive." Their motto became "change everything, except for my wife and kids." In its products, Samsung tried to change its emphasis from quantity to quality. For instance, Samsung Electronics recalled 150,000 cordless phones in 1995 after receiving a report that many malfunctioned. The recalled items were then destroyed with hammers and burned in front of production workers.

Also, to reform executives and employees' obsession with quantitative growth and to encourage their creativity, Samsung implemented the so-called 7.4 system. The idea was to let employees come to work at seven in the morning and leave at four in the afternoon, instead of working from eight thirty to six, giving them free time to develop themselves. Lee dismissed executives who advocated quantitative growth, and he sought to instill a culture of quality throughout the organization. This initiative helped Samsung Electronics weather the foreign exchange crisis that Korea faced in 1997. The crisis was a wake-up call to Korean firms. The stock market crashed, and many highly leveraged firms and banks that provided loans to them went bankrupt. All large business groups including Samsung had to lower their debts by divesting underperforming businesses and becoming more efficient. Subsequent to the crisis, Samsung Group got rid of 20 of its 65 subsidiaries. It also liquidated 236 businesses and dismissed about 50,000 employees. Samsung Group's debt to equity ration went down from 370% in 1996 to 193% in 1999.

In June 2003, Samsung Group launched the second phase of the New Management Movement. At that time, "genius management," "discovery of future growth momentum," and "focus on the Chinese market" were selected as core business mottos. "Genius management" refers to an initiative to foster and bring in creative talent. In this context, Chairman Lee encouraged Samsung's business division presidents to attract creative engineers and managers from outside the firm.

The New Management Movement contrasts with Jack Welch's management initiatives at GE. During this time, Samsung switched its role model from Japanese *keiretsus*, having their own big problems at that time, to GE. In fact, Chairman Lee maintains close contact with Jack Welch. GE's campaign began with business restructuring under the slogan of "selling any business if not number one or number two in terms of global market share," and led to a workout program that would shake up both the organization and employees' mindsets. Samsung began by changing its employees' mindsets, implementing new systems and slogans, and then proceeded to restructuring. These differences occurred because there were many limitations on restructuring in Korea, such as liquidating companies, and therefore it was critical to change mindsets first. Chairman Lee's movement became crucial for Samsung Electronics' quantum leap from being an obscure second-tier firm that produced cheap, generic products to being a globally recognized leader in innovation.

# 5

# Wannabe Globals

Our local HQs at U.S., Europe and Asia should present a new goal for localization. But this process should be in harmony with a unified goal, making Sony into a truly global enterprise. I will set global localization as our future principle from now on. This is a new way for Sony; Sony will suffice local demand through localization and develop globalization and technologies at the same time.

*—The late Akio Morita, co-founder of Sony*[1]

The problem Samsung Group is facing can be summarized in one line: Samsung Group's speed of globalization exceeds that of Samsung Group's globalization capability.

*—Yong-wook Jeon, Jung-hwa Han,*
*Authors of* Toward a First-class Enterprise[2]

This chapter focuses on Sony and Samsung Electronics' globalization efforts, which have been key to both firms' strategies. There are several ways of looking at globalization. If globalization means producing goods in a country with the cheapest costs, selling them in the most profitable places, and operating business all over the world, Sony and Samsung Electronics are both globalized. Yet, because both firms' decision-making power is concentrated in their home countries, it is more accurate to say these firms are still globalizing.

## Sony's Global Strategy

### Global Localization Strategy

When Sony began trying to grow the U.S. market, Morita took charge of Sony's U.S. subsidiary. In his book *Made in Japan*, Morita discussed how he responded to an antidumping lawsuit against Sony by appointing a local attorney, and actively promoted localization by recruiting local managers. Mr. Morita was Sony's first expatriate manager. He rented an apartment on Fifth Avenue in Manhattan in 1962, and tried to assimilate. He even asked his wife to have more American friends than Japanese. Most of Sony's other senior managers also worked abroad at some point. Idei founded Sony's French operation, and Sony's former President Ando led business expansion in the United States.

From early on, Sony believed it was important to secure local managers. It constructed a TV production factory in Rancho Bernardo, California, in 1972 and a color TV factory in Wales in 1974. In 1972, Sony appointed Harvey Shein from CBS Records as the President of Sony America. Shein taught Sony how to save money and enhance efficiency to generate more revenue. According to Morita, "He Americanized the company totally and did a fine job of it. He recruited a new group of top executives and fired some of the previous group, and he installed a budgeting system that kept tight financial control of everything. He even flew economy class himself when he traveled on domestic flights. He considered cost in everything, and as far as profit is concerned, there was no match for him."[3] Sony was the first Japanese firm to issue ADRs on the New York Stock Exchange (NYSE) in 1961, raising 1.2 billion yen; to issue consolidated financial statements according to U.S. accounting standards (GAAP); and to be listed on the NYSE in 1970.

In the late 1980s, as the yen doubled in value against the dollar, it became difficult for Sony to produce exports in Japan. With an appreciated yen, local manufacturing and local sourcing became more attractive. This was a time when Japanese firms were in a shopping spree all over the world. Mitsubishi Real Estate bought Rockefeller Center in 1989, which epitomized the Japanese acquisitions of U.S. icons. Other Japanese companies followed suit, and Sony was no exception. In 1987, Sony built a factory in Singapore, producing laser pick-ups for CD players, followed by further construction in Malaysia, Thailand, and Indonesia. In the United States, Sony acquired a semiconductor factory in San Antonio in 1989, and built a CRT and color TV factory in Pittsburgh in 1993. In 1997, Sony constructed a factory for producing TV glass jointly with Asahi and Corning in Pittsburg.

Morita established Operation Headquarters (OHQs) in four regions, including Japan, the United States, Europe, and Southeast Asia. For example, Sony Europe, established in Germany, and administrating the overall European region, was headed by Jacob Schmuckli, the president of Sony Germany. SONIS in Singapore became Sony's HQ for Southeast Asia. Sony delegated most decisions to the OHQs, which handled production, sales, logistics, technology, and financing in ways that accounted for local needs. Sony HQ remained only as the world headquarters, overseeing the firm from a global perspective, and being the hub for overall research and development. Morita dubbed this the Global Localization strategy. His idea was to have an optimal balance between localization and globalization. In other words, localization, satisfying local demand, should proceed in harmony with Sony's overall global strategy. A famous motto, which both Sony and other large multinationals pursued at that time, was "Think Globally, Act Locally."

Sony showed its commitment to treat individuals according to their ability, regardless of their nationality. It also established political connections with influential people in the United States, such as Henry Kissinger, the former U.S. secretary of state, and used them as lobbyists. In 1992, Sony appointed Peter Peterson as its outside director. Peterson had been chairman of the Blackstone Group and was a former economic advisor to the president in the Nixon administration.

The level of Sony's globalization varied by business area. For example, Sony's music and film business was controlled by its U.S. subsidiary and was managed almost entirely by local managers. The HQ for the mobile communication business was relocated in London, after it was merged into a joint venture with Ericsson. The audio, games, semiconductors, and component divisions have their HQs in Japan and are controlled mostly by Japanese managers.

Sony's computer division is by far the most globalized of all its hardware businesses. With its operations in San Diego, it is run by managers who have a global vision and mindset. In contrast, authority for the TV, devices, and material businesses is still largely concentrated in Japan and has the traditional Japanese corporate culture.

Under Sony's global organization, there are country managers for each nation. Interestingly, Sony has separate production and sales organizations; regional organizations take charge only of marketing and sales, but all of Sony's factories are controlled by a separate organization, SEMC. For example, the Sony subsidiary in Korea is merely a sales organization, and its factories are controlled by SEMC. Country managers do not possess much decision-making power.

### Losing Control over Overseas Subsidiaries

While pursuing its Global Localization strategy and delegating decision-making power to local managers, Sony has emphasized that "Sony is ONE." It has tried to make local managers adhere to Sony's management principles and basic policies. Many questions remain, however, as to whether Sony can control its local managers by emphasizing its management principles while it simultaneously pursues localization and delegates decision-making power. After all, "Think Globally, Act Locally" is easier to say than to practice.

Sony's main overseas market was the United States. Under Shein, Sony America's sales increased from $300 million to $750 million between 1972 and 1978. Sony planned to launch an active sales campaign to sell the Betamax VCR in the U.S. market in 1975, but Shein and his cadre of local managers hesitated to invest in promotion because they believed too much advertising would undermine their profits. Morita once called Shein in the middle of the night and yelled at him, "If you are not going to spend a million or two million dollars on the Betamax campaign in the next two months, I will fire you."[4] To Morita, the local U.S. managers appeared to be interested only in short-term profits and neglected to invest in advertising that was essential for long-term sales.

Mickey Schulhof, who spearheaded the acquisition of CBS Records and Columbia Pictures, was Shein's successor at Sony America. He was criticized for operating Sony America too independently from Sony's HQ and for failing to maintain control over Columbia Pictures. Under the two managers he recruited to head Sony (Columbia) Pictures, Jon Peters and Peter Guber, new movies went way over budget and were generally unsuccessful.[5] Because Sony America was the parent company to Sony Pictures, it was under Schulhof's jurisdiction, and Sony's HQ staff could not intervene even though it was apparent that Schulhof had lost control. Because of the autonomy that Schulhof enjoyed, it was practically impossible to create the synergies between the hardware and software businesses that Morita had initially envisioned. Even if Sony's electronics business tried to create synergies with the music or film business, it could not do so unless the terms were agreeable to U.S. management.

During Schulhof's tenure, Sony America often revolted against Sony HQ's decisions and frequently made decisions unilaterally. For example, when PlayStation was released, all the mangers in Sony America's game business were game professionals whose experience was based on Nintendo's business model. Sony America opposed PlayStation's grey and purple-tinted design, and ordered a white-colored product solely for the U.S. market. Local managers also thought the controller was too small, and wanted to change the name PlayStation, saying it made people think of Playboy. Moreover, they insisted on setting the price in the United States and proposed one as high as Nintendo's. The essence of PlayStation, however, was its global standard, one design with one price. PlayStation was also a game platform with an innovative concept that could overturn the existing game industry. Finally, President Kutaragi of Sony Computer Entertainment deprived Sony America of its control over PlayStation. He set up its own local corporation in San Francisco, replaced all local managers, and instituted a new management team. Sony used large store chains such as Wal-Mart, KMart, and Toys"R"Us as its major distribution channel, instead of resorting to the traditional electronics retailers where Nintendo was based. Subsequently, PlayStation became an unprecedented hit in the U.S. as well as in Japan.

Sony HQ also overrode Sony America's ideas about VAIO computers. The color of VAIO, with magnesium compound and violet, targeted the advanced U.S. market. Local managers asserted that the color and the futuristic design would not appeal to conservative U.S. consumers, and also opposed the name, saying that it was difficult to pronounce. Based on their market research, they proposed "Sony

Personal Computer" as the name. In the end, Sony HQ used the name VAIO to sell PCs in the United States. Sony HQ also changed the name of the movie theater chain that came with the Columbia Pictures acquisitions back from Sony Theaters to Loews, because the rundown theaters in many locations could tarnish Sony's brand image.

Some of Sony America's frequent conflicts with Sony HQ may have originated from differences in culture or ways of thinking, but the main reason was that Sony was incapable of controlling local operations while Morita pursued global localization. In other words, the hypothetical balance between globalization and localization was broken because of Sony's limited ability to offer global control. Because only a small number of individuals, such as Morita and Ohga, controlled Sony at a worldwide level, the firm did not have the organizational infrastructure to control local managers. Morita and Ohga instead managed local corporations based on their personal relationships. For instance, they trusted Schulhof, and gave him full power over Sony America. This meant that the only possible way to control Sony America was to control Schulhof, which only Morita and Ohga could do. This system ceased to function when the personal relationships between Schulhof and Morita and Ohga grew stronger, and Morita and Ohga could not control Schulhof.

Idei, who succeeded Ohga as president in 1994, once said: "They were all in cahoots— Burak, Pete Peterson, Mickey [Schulhof]—each of them was doing his job responsibility as an individual, but together as a group it seemed to me they were very skillful at working the generous entity called Sony. The problem was, we had never truly dealt with foreigners. When they recommended something we would generally accept the recommendation. I had done lots of business in the U.S. and Europe and I could see these people taking advantage of relationships to move the company to expend funds. They would all act together in this. Japanese of the generation before me had an inferiority complex about foreigners. Akio Morita himself was a living inferiority complex."[6] Idei also commented that "Mickey Schulhof was enjoying both the privileges of an American executive, the power and the salary, and the ambiguity of Japanese corporate governance. He was skimming the cream off the top of both worlds."[7] These episodes show the problems in Sony's governance structure for overseas subsidiaries, its management style, which attempted to mix Japanese and American practices, did not work out. Schulhof was dismissed in 1995. It is said that the employees at Sony HQ applauded when they heard he was leaving.[3]

When Idei came into office, Sony's global localization strategy faced an inevitable change. Idei announced that he would not pursue globalization for its own sake and that transferring power to the local manager wasn't always desirable. Looking at Sony America, he argued that Sony emphasized localization excessively as it implemented its global localization strategy. He believed the global headquarters should play a stronger role, and shifted power back to it. He also made himself Sony America's CEO to reinforce control of the Japanese HQ over overseas subsidiaries.

### Excessive Investment in the Bubble Period

From the mid-1980s to the early 1990s, Sony's overseas production facilities were not necessarily built in order to achieve cost advantages. In some cases, it cost more to produce locally. Sony's global localization strategy was designed to develop products that best suited local market conditions, and so justify premium prices. Costs were a secondary issue. Further, the yen's appreciation during this period made it impossible to stick to producing in Japan and exporting to other countries. As the yen appreciated, the price of overseas assets converted into yen became cheaper, which made most of Sony's overseas investments too excessive. Sony also invested in many unrelated businesses, such as real estate.

Overseas investments during this period greatly expanded Sony's production capacity. But this increased capacity could pose risks if it was not supported by sales increases. With the digitalization of consumer electronics, it became more difficult to differentiate products, and Sony found it harder to maintain its price premium. Cost savings became increasingly important. From the mid-1990s onward, as its consumer electronics business deteriorated, Sony had to reevaluate all overseas production. It began to liquidate its overseas facilities, including several semiconductor plants and its CRT factory in Pittsburgh. This restructuring was facilitated as Sony reorganized its businesses into a company structure to improve its financial health. In 2003, Sony announced a restructuring plan, called "Transformation 60," to reduce its headcount by 20,000 and to shut down 20 manufacturing plants worldwide. This restructuring is still going on.

## Samsung's Globalization Strategy

### Electronics Complex and Regional HQ System

Until the early 1990s, Samsung Electronics' level of globalization was quite limited. It produced OEM products in Korea and exported them. Although it had local sales subsidiaries that were set up in bigger markets such as America and Europe, it relied on indirect sales in smaller markets through its the general trading company of its group affiliate, Samsung Corporation.

When Chairman Lee launched the New Management Movement in 1993, he pushed to globalize Samsung Group. One part of this initiative involved constructing electronics manufacturing complexes in other countries. It created five complexes, which were built to create various synergies, such as sharing local knowledge, saving labor costs, jointly purchase some components, and quickly diagnosing management problems, by colocating the subsidiaries of Samsung Group's electronics companies. Samsung relocated some of its subsidiaries' production plants to its Tijuana complex. For instance, Samsung Electro-mechanics and Samsung SDI's production subsidiaries moved into the complex in 1995. In March 1996, Samsung Electronics' other production plant moved into the complex, closing down its other location in Tijuana. In 1997, Samsung built monitor plant number two and constructed another plant for Samsung Electro-mechanics in 1998. As of 2006, SAMEX, Samsung Electronics at Tijuana Complex, is producing color TVs, color monitors, and mobile phones. This complex connected the entire value chain, from parts and components manufacturing to the sales of completed products. In this way, Samsung reduced its logistics costs, because the time required to supply parts was reduced, and overall it saved an estimated $7 million by conducting other supporting activities jointly, such as customs clearances, purchasing, tax, promotions, and logistics. Samsung wanted to use this complex as a beachhead for expanding further into North, Central, and South America. Other complexes were located in Selemban, Malaysia; Winyard, UK; Tianjin, China; and Manaus, Brazil. Samsung Electronics' other production facilities that did not become part of the complexes were also advised to co-locate with each other to exploit the synergies between them. For example, SEIN, the Indonesian subsidiary producing VCRs, DVDs, ODDs, and color TVs, attracted its group-affiliated supplier, Samsung Electro-mechanics, to relocate in its vicinity in order to ensure swift supply of parts. SEPHIL, Samsung Electronics' Philippine subsidiary, established in 2001, settled right next to the already-existing Samsung Electric's Philippine subsidiary, receiving much help in settling down based on the experiences of the existing subsidiaries.

Because Samsung Group, including Samsung Electronics, had accelerated its overseas expansion when it initiated the New Management Movement, it implemented a regional HQ system in 1996 to enhance the efficiency of its complexes and transfer decision making to overseas subsidiaries. The overseas HQs included five regional HQs located in Japan, China, Europe, America, and Southeast Asia, and three smaller regional HQs in Central/Southern America, Russia and CIS (Commonwealth of Independent States), and the Middle East. Samsung Group's affiliates in the electronics, financial/insurance, chemistry, machinery, and other industries had already pursued globalization and set up their own overseas subsidiaries.

The regional HQ system was intended to let the regional HQs function as the Samsung Group headquarters in that region. The system was supposed to create synergies by integrating the administration of Samsung Group's affiliates' various subsidiaries, thus accelerating communication and decision making, and enabling these headquarters to capitalize on their understanding of local markets by seeking new business opportunities. Under the system, each regional headquarters would make decisions regarding local activities such as production and sales and would be responsible for local profitability. The responsibilities of the HQs in Korea would be limited to the domestic market,

### Problems of Excessive Localization

The initial results of this more decentralized structure were very disappointing. Some of Samsung's overseas operations were unprofitable and/or too expensive to continue production at their current locations. Because every Samsung subsidiary in a complex paid the same wages, production costs for some subsidiaries were higher than they would have been had these subsidiaries located elsewhere. Actual synergies were limited because each business unit's characteristics were different. Companies that had very different businesses, such as electronics, insurance, and trading, were all controlled by the regional HQ, which only raised the complexity and merely added another layer of hierarchy rather than create synergies. Many considered this to be the main reason for breaking up the regional HQ system. The depreciation of the Korean won against other major currencies during the financial crisis in Korea further exacerbated these problems. Samsung Electronics ended up closing down its factory in Winyard in 1998 and moved it to Hungary, where Samsung SDI produced picture tubes. Samsung Electronics built a microwave factory at the Tijuana complex in 1998, but the completed factory remained idle because as the Korean won became weaker after the financial crisis it became much cheaper to produce in Korea and then export.

These results caused many employees in Samsung Group to reject the "integration strategy." Some even said that there was a "minus" synergy. A manager in Samsung Electronics said that "because electric parts don't cost much to transport, and don't need much ongoing investment, there wasn't much to gain by being located in the complex. The only synergy we experienced was cheaper transportation costs, but even those didn't matter much. It was possible to closely share information, because the customers—subsidiaries—were close by, but that isn't so different from what we do in Korea. Rather, we ended up paying a higher salary for workers by colocating with all other Samsung affiliates"[9] In the complexes, all the important positions were filled by Korean expatriate managers. To their way of thinking, localization meant anything beyond manufacturing locally. The complexes were not truly localized, however; they did not hire local managers, secure local resources, or capitalize on opportunities to learn indigenous management know-how. Instead, because Samsung Electronics' local subsidiaries dealt only with other Samsung subsidiaries located in the same complex, Samsung Electronics merely transferred its vertical integration system to a foreign country.

At last, complaints about the negative synergies of these operations led to dissolution of the regional HQ system. A manager working at an overseas corporation commented: "The regional HQ's job was to find new business opportunities or do some creative work that could not be pursued from HQs located in Korea. The problem was that the regional

HQs focused more on financial controls than they did on finding new business opportunities."[10] Samsung's deployment of the regional HQ system at the group level added complexity and contributed to this system's eventual collapse because it tried to harmonize local business practices among subsidiaries in a vast variety of industries.

### Return to a Global Organization

After Samsung Group's regional HQ system was dissolved, Samsung Electronics restructured into a Global Product Manager (GPM) organization in 1998. The GPM organization structure comprised 17 business divisions such as TVs, VCRs, mobile communications, and so forth. Each took charge of global production and sales organization for its products at the Korean HQ, and the GPM head located in Korea made all important decisions regarding strategies, technical support, pricing, and production scheduling, and had bottom-line responsibility.

The local organizations executed a GPM's decisions according to local conditions. A manager commented on this plan: "The GPM system would be difficult to work if the products radically differed in each nation, but Samsung Electronics' products are mostly global. There's no need to make different products for each nation, and there's not much need for localization. I think the current GPM system is fine. Some small differences according to each market can be made easily by using different parts. The designs remain the same. The pricing decision is made by GPMs at the HQ, and all I have to do is focus on enhancing productivity. My goal is simply to increase the productivity and save more on material costs."[11]

Others, however, believed that the GPM system was insensitive to local needs. A local manager pointed out, "The past European HQ system developed marketing strategies that took local conditions into consideration such as local management, promotion and education. Especially in Europe, the industrial relations issue had to be managed in a comprehensive way, encompassing the entire European region by having a multi-national corporate form rather than let each nation manage its own problems; so, we made the Samsung New Management Committee, which could be considered as the solution, and dealt with the industrial relations issues in the overall European region. But now, the whole system is centralized, moving just as the GPM instructs, and manufacturing subsidiaries have to follow GPMs' orders regarding production quantity or pricing. Therefore, it has grown more difficult for the GPM system to respond to local conditions."[12] Some managers noted another problem: "We are now centralized again under the GPM organization. The GPM heads tend to be engineers who built up their careers in production and design centers. Their primary concern is to increase production efficiency. They do not know much about sales, or they don't have any experience running business overseas. They can manage the sales of existing products, but might not be able to invest in new products or build distribution channels."[13] Another problem of the GPM system was that local subsidiaries became cost centers rather than profit centers, and thus lost the incentive to develop new products or open new markets.

Samsung Electronics changed the organization structure again in 2001 from GPM to GBM (Global Business Manager). GBM is almost equivalent to GPM, but uses "business" rather than "product" to widen managers' perspectives from a focus on products to a focus on the whole industry. The change was supposed to widen the scope of products that are produced and sold by the divisions and to induce divisions to achieve maximum profit while optimizing the global management system.

## Problems with External Globalization

### External Globalization

Sony has a history of expanding overseas that is much longer than Samsung Electronics'. Sony has many overseas production plants in locations worldwide. It has many foreign outside directors on its board. The fact that a foreigner, Howard Stringer, was appointed as Sony's CEO demonstrates the firm's intention to globalize further.

Nonetheless, it is uncertain whether Sony is capable of operating a global organization. Morita and Ohga were very competent global managers, but Sony's organizational-level capability may be limited, which lets local subsidiaries get completely out of control. Moreover, Sony's globalization may reflect Morita's hubris and arrogance, his desire to expand overseas in order to show the world that "Sony is the only Japanese company that is capable of global management," even though Sony lacked the infrastructure to manage the challenges of globalization. It is also legitimate to ask whether Sony is currently globalized enough to deal with a foreign CEO, and whether Stringer truly functions as a CEO, or is merely a temporary CEO whose role is very limited.

Samsung Electronics trails Sony in every aspect of globalization and is not seriously trying to be less Korean-centered. It has perceived globalization merely as building overseas factories and producing abroad, buying parts from local sources, and hiring locals for jobs with limited responsibility in its sales organizations. Under the current GBM system, most of the overseas corporations merely follow the instructions given by the HQ. In short, its version of globalization has been defensive and inward-looking. In contrast to Sony, which conducts its major meetings in English, and does the same in smaller meetings if a single foreigner is present, Samsung Electronics' attempt to use English as its official language was short-lived. Everyone, including the president, had to write down and read what he wanted to say, and the plan was soon abandoned.

**Securing Global Managers**

In the United States and Europe, Sony has secured many local managers, but in Asia and other developing countries, Japanese expatriates still occupy major posts. The expatriates are managed by the country manager, but important strategic decisions are reported to more senior managers of each division in Japan. This structure means that country managers evaluate the expatriates, but do not have actual power or control over them.

Ando promoted a project, "Global Open Architecture," which focused on identifying 100 important posts all around the world, and on hiring foreigners to fill them. Its aim was to hire talented people from outside sources, regardless of their nationality or gender, instead of hiring internally. Ando and Idei believed that Sony could not globalize adequately or pursue its network strategy unless competent foreign managers could be brought in.

In contrast, virtually all the heads of Samsung Electronics' local operations have been Korean. Samsung Group believed that it needed managers with global mindsets in order to achieve "globalization" as defined by its "New Management Movement," and it has been using a "local specialist" system in which it develops its existing personnel into global managers. Nonetheless, it has not placed full confidence in local managers, or sufficiently delegated power to them. The policy of relying on internal recruits, especially Korean ones, has helped the firm achieve discipline and swift execution, but it has also greatly undermined the firm's capability to respond sensitively to local market demands. For instance, local managers are not empowered since all the important decisions have to be communicated back to the head office in Korea, often only in Korean. Korean expatriates can grab a phone and explain at length what they need to their counterparts in HQ. As a consequence, a lower-level expatriate manager has often more influence over his or her locally hired superior. Even outside hires are mostly Korean-Americans, who not only know the U.S. market but can also communicate with Korean expatriates in their mother language and who have a more favorable attitude toward Korea.

Samsung Electronics has succeeded thus far with its Korean-centric bias, but it is unclear whether that policy will continue to work. As discussed above, Samsung Electronics has relied substantially on Koreans who have studied in the United States for its R&D and technology. If Samsung Electronics wishes to remain a technological leader, it cannot restrict itself in this way. This kind of talent is always in short supply. Samsung also needs more managers who have global perspectives and must build a system that can utilize talent from all over the world. Moreover, although the Korean culture's emphasis on hierarchy and rote memorization may facilitate swift, effective strategy execution, this same emphasis may obstruct the expression of creative ideas or dissenting opinions. For Samsung Electronics to become a true industrial leader, its leaders must recruit people from other countries who have diverse opinions and creative ideas.

In addition, Samsung Electronics must acquire other firms to gain advanced know-how to speed up its technological progress. To prepare for this effort, it must learn the basic techniques for overseas mergers and acquisitions (M&A). The GBM organizations also need to develop the ability to respond to local demands. Otherwise, it will be difficult for the company to face the challenges of globalization.

In short, Samsung Electronics is still in its fledgling phase of globalization, and it has not experienced the true challenges of this process. Unlike Sony, it has not fully encountered either the need for, or limitations of, global management. Insofar as Samsung Electronics wants to become a global leader rather than remain a follower, its inexperience in managing global operations and in attracting global resources may be its weakest link.

# Part 2 Organizational Process and Leadership

# 6

# Same Silos
# but Different Outcomes

We also embarked on a review of the corporate organization, in particular the traditional pyramid model, and management systems, namely the command and control–based systems. In doing so, we decided to create a network-based organizational structure. Specifically, the transfer of a wide scope of authority will promote the autonomous management of each business and facilitate swifter decision making. At the same time, under the leadership of the Sony Group Headquarters, we will bolster strategic alliances among the five pillars and formulate integrated group-wide strategies with the view to maximizing corporate value. We call this new management model "integrated/decentralized management."

*–Nobuyuki Idei, former CEO of Sony*[1]

Samsung Electronics reminds me of a military organization. It has a clear hierarchy with orders and obedience, and there is a tension felt in the overall organization. It is an organization full of people who are ready to rush towards the frontline and sacrifice themselves with an order of a commanding officer. Chairman Kun-hee Lee is the commander in chief of this military organization.

*–A high-ranked executive at Sony*

Much evidence may suggest that Sony's recent stagnation and Samsung Electronics' fast rise result from differences in their key strategies in technology, marketing, and globalization. The major decisions made in these functional aspects, however, are actually based on the management systems of the two companies: the company culture and the organizational structure. In other words, organization processes matter more than firms' strategies themselves would do in explaining the differences in the firms' performance.

Many modern companies use a multidivisional structure, in which divisional managers make operating decisions for their divisions, and top executives at the corporate level make only strategic decisions. Companies structured along product lines tend to have product divisions, and companies diversified geographically usually have area divisions. With their various product groups, Sony and Samsung Electronics both have product divisions. Sony also implemented a company structure in which individual product divisions have separate balance sheets and income statements, and operate almost like independent companies. The divisional structure offers clear accountability, but individual divisions can become too independent under it. Sometimes product divisions in the same firm are "silos": they compete with each other rather than cooperate. They can even refuse to share resources or transfer technology to each other. In fact, Sony's "company system" structure precipitated the firm's stagnation. Similarly, Samsung Electronics' rigid organizational structure and company culture have been both a source of key capabilities in the commodities sector and a hindrance to product development, for which originality and creativity are essential.

## Sony's Company Structure

### The Culture of Freedom and Openness
Freedom and open-mindedness have long been the foundation for Sony's corporate culture and organizing principles. Ibuka's founding statement of purpose clearly states the guiding maxim of its corporate culture. "Let's make a company where everyone feels happy to work." During new employee training, Morita used to tell recruits that, "We did not draft you. This is not the army, so that means you have voluntarily

chosen Sony. This is your responsibility, and normally if you join this company we expect that you will stay for the next 20 or 30 years. Nobody can live twice, and the next 20 or 30 years is the brightest period of your life. You only get it once. When you leave the company 30 years from now or when your life is finished, I do not want you to regret that you spent all those years here. That would be tragedy. I cannot stress the point too much that this is your responsibility to yourself. So I say to you, the most important thing in the next few months is for you to decide whether you will be happy or unhappy here. So even though we recruited you, we cannot, as management, or a third party, make other people happy; happiness must be created yourself."[2]

Sony also began an "internal recruiting system" soon after it was founded. When a division or a project team posted the qualifications for a new job, employees could apply without telling their bosses. The company believed employees should develop their capabilities and · realize their potential. This made talent sharing possible within Sony.

Sony also practiced on-the-job training (OJT). It sent new employees straight to its business units without any formal training because it believed employees could best enhance their skills when they faced real work and that they would grow most when they had to accomplish a job that at first was beyond their ability. Sony even introduced a recruiting system that did not require a potential employee to reveal what university he had gone to, so that its managers would look for talent without being biased by a school's name.

In 1988, Sony also began hiring mid-career people from outside the firm. Ibuka said, "We need to transfuse heterogenous blood, not pure blood, so that we strengthen our organization and further develop the corporate culture that is Sony."[3] Outstanding foreign employees were hired for key positions that would facilitate global localization. Sony's organization became horizontal, not hierarchical or authoritarian. When Sony developed a new product, individuals voluntarily formed a horizontal team and disbanded after finishing the project.

Like most Japanese companies, Sony gave its divisional managers much latitude. The Japanese word, *Genba*, means that field managers should be the ultimate decision makers. Despite the independence of its business units, however, organizational conflict used to be minimal. The CEOs of Sony's founding generation, like Ibuka, Morita, and Ohga, managed Sony through charismatic leadership. No one would object, for instance, to Morita's decisions, even if he or she might have held different views.

### The Introduction of a Company System

In 1983, Sony began using a "business group system," which was a kind of product division structure. Divisional managers had authority and responsibility over operations, sales, and profitability. In 1994, when Idei was elected president, Sony introduced a "company system" in order to bolster earnings and improve its balance sheet, which had ballooned with debt during the previous decade.

Sony's financial condition was very bad at that time. Large foreign acquisitions such as Columbia Pictures and investments in foreign manufacturing plants under the global localization strategy were financed by substantial debt (see Figure 6.1). Sony's consolidated total assets increased more than three times: from 1.6 trillion yen in 1987 to 4.9 trillion yen in 1992, and its interest-bearing debts increased

*Figure 6.1*    Sony's Interest-Bearing Debts and Debt Equity Ratio

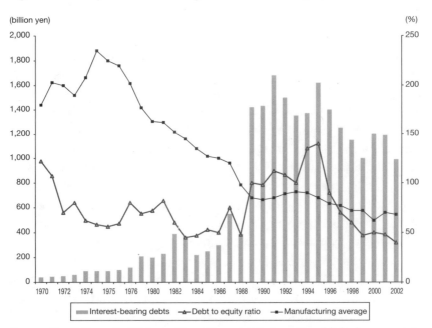

*Source:* Iba, T. From the History of Sony Financial Strategy. Unpublished manuscript, 2003, p. 47

from 340 billion yen in 1987 to 1.7 trillion yen in 1992.[4] Profits from the electronics business deteriorated from 1991 to 1993 because of the yen's high value, and Sony's credit rating fell from AA in 1988 to A in 1993. Columbia Pictures' accumulated losses of $3.5 billion had to be written off in 1994. Sony had to improve its financial performance and pay down debts.

The company system initiative reinforced the business group system, but it also made each operating division assume responsibility for balance sheet items such as production facilities and other assets. The company president had the right to invest up to a certain threshold and to manage headcount. A company system creates a virtual spinoff organization that makes individual business divisions take responsibility as if they were independent companies. Ohga asked each company president to manage his business as if he was the owner. This is how he outlined the goals of the company system:[5]

1. To enhance core businesses while developing new ones
2. To introduce an organizational structure through which sales and production would work closely together and respond quickly to market changes
3. To simplify the structure in order to clarify responsibilities and transfer authority so that responses to external changes would be quick
4. To reduce the level of hierarchy in the organization
5. To encourage entrepreneurial spirit in order to foster a dynamic management base for the twenty-first century

Under the company system, Sony HQ was supposed to be like a holding company that would take responsibility only for investing in new businesses and overall coordination. Sony's 19 business divisions were reorganized into eight "companies": Consumer A&V; Components; Recording Media & Energy; Broadcast; Business & Industrial Systems; InfoCom; Mobile Electronics; and Semiconductors. Sony's game, music, movie, and insurance business was managed as separate organizations.

The company system, along with the effort to cut costs and improve profits, helped Sony improve its performance substantially and to reduce its debt. In its 1993 fiscal year, Sony's sales and profits were 3.7 trillion yen and 100 billion yen, respectively, and its net profit was just 15.3 billion yen. In its 1997 fiscal year, Sony's sales were 6.7 trillion yen, operating profit was 500 billion yen, and net profit was 202 billion yen. Sony also trimmed its level of interest-paying debt to 130 million yen by its 1997 fiscal year.

### Changes in the Company Organization
Sony has modified its company structure several times since 1994. In 1998, the eight companies were reorganized into ten companies. In April 1999, these ten companies were integrated into three: the Home Network Company, the Personal IT Network Company, and the Core Technology & Network Company. Moving from ten individual companies to three broadly defined Network Companies represented substantial change in how decisions were made within Sony. This reorganization reflected Idei's network concept. He thought the ten companies were too narrowly defined to create synergies through "integrated/decentralized management." For example, the IT Company, which made VAIO computers, and the Personal Mobile Communicaion Company, which included the mobile phone and digital camera business, were combined into the Personal IT Network Company. Each "network company" had another level below it. At this lower level, there were 25 small, independent "companies," which were similar to business divisions. R&D functions were transferred from Sony's HQ to the three network companies. A separate ad hoc organization, called Digital Network Solutions (DNS), was set up under the group HQ to develop new network businesses, such as So-net, an Internet access provider, and digital content businesses, such as ones that provided movies, music, and financial services through the network. In 2000, the broadcasting business under the Home Network Company was transferred into DNS, and the Communication System Network Solutions Company was established, increasing the number of network companies to four.

In 2001, Sony reversed its decision to group individual companies into more broadly defined network companies. This time, Sony reorganized these four network companies into seven network companies. The Displays business was spun off from Home Network Company, Personal IT Network Company was divided into Mobile Network Company and Digital Telecommunication Network Company,

*Figure 6.2* Changes in Sony's Organizational Structure

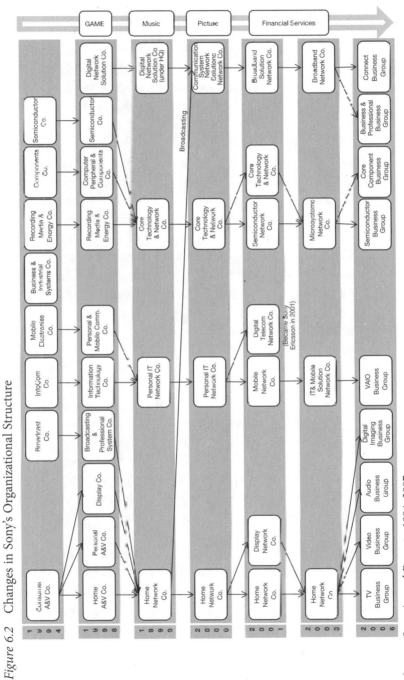

*Source:* Sony Annual Reports, 1994–2007.

and Core Technology & Network Company was separated into a Semiconductor Network Company and Core Technology Network Company. In 2003, there was another reversal in the organizing principle. This time, these seven network companies were consolidated back into four network companies: Home Networks Company, IT& Mobile Solution Networks Company, Broadband Networks Company, and Micro Systems Networks Company. In effect, Sony reversed its previous decision to break four network companies into seven just two years before. (See Figure 6.2.)

There did not seem to be a consistent objective for this repeated restructuring. After Idei and Ando resigned, and Stringer and Chubachi became CEO and president in 2005, Sony returned to the business group system that it had used a decade earlier. Sony's current organizational structure is shown in Figure 6.3. In 2007, Sony's nine business divisions were TV, Video, Audio, Digital Imaging, Business & Professional, VAIO, Semiconductors, Core Components, and Connect.

The restructuring reflected Idei's network strategy, which involved creating a Big Bang by connecting and integrating Sony's several businesses in order to find opportunities for a quantum leap into new businesses. Idei explained that he wanted to introduce "complexity theory" into management. According to him, "The business domains of Sony extend beyond electronics to include games, music, pictures, insurance, and other fields. To make these businesses function smoothly, a bottom-up and a top-down strategy must be implemented simultaneously and interactively. A bottom-up strategy comes from each business unit, and a top-down strategy from the head office. Sony is an organization made up of many elements. We must adhere to the concept of 'a complex system,' in which the various elements interact with each other to create new values and make the whole greater than the sum of its parts."[6] It is possible that Idei was a pioneer who was experimenting with a new way of organizing business. In some sense, Idei's experiments are reminiscent of the gospel of the New Economy during the IT bubble, when pundits argued that old, slow brick–and-mortar firms would be replaced by nimble Internet startups. "Complexity management" was just another management fad.[7] His frequent experiments, however, worsened pre-existing problems in Sony's organizational structure.

*Figure 6.3* Sony's Organizational Structure in 2007

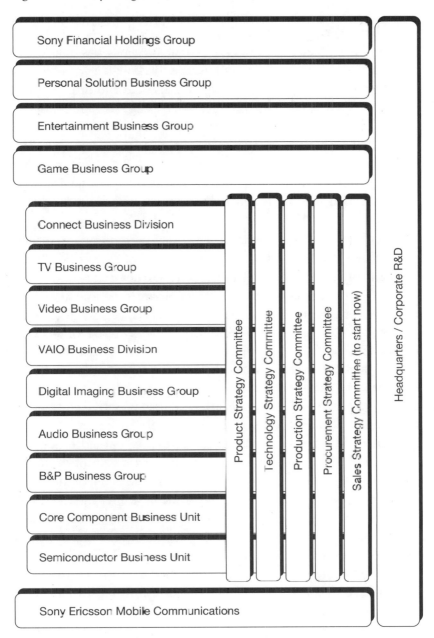

*Source:* Sony Annual Report 2007.

## Problem with Sony's Organizational Structure

### Short-Term Performance and Legacy

Ever since it adopted a business group structure, Sony has thoroughly reviewed the performance of each business division. If a division with sales higher than 100 billion yen achieved its sales and profit targets, its managers were given targets such as increasing sales and profits by more than 10%, achieving 10% profitability, as measured by ordinary income divided by sales, improving cash flow by more than ten billion yen, and achieving other market share objectives. Before the company system was introduced, the evaluation was heavily weighted toward sales and profits, and the weight on balance sheet items, such as cash flow, was less than 20%.[8]

Under the company system, however, each company was evaluated annually by Sony HQ as if it were a company listed on the stock market. Besides being responsible for meeting their predetermined sales and profitability targets, company presidents began to be evaluated to a much greater extent on their divisions' balance sheets.[9] ROI (Return on investment) based on cash flow analysis was required for any new investment. HQ set a 10% capital cost for individual companies, so the ROI had to exceed this hurdle. Managers thus had to be very sensitive about the payback period for new investments. It was a great cultural shock to them since in the past they had preferred any kind of investment in their divisions, since they did not have to pay for such investment. In other words, the more investment would have been the better since they could crank out higher sales and profits from the investment. After they had to pay for such investment out of their own pocket, they became more conscious of the cost of capital. In 1998, Sony also began emphasizing shareholder value, and included various measures related to shareholder value (increases against the previous year, the ratio of goal achievement, the return on invested capital). These became the most important evaluation measures.[10] Sony also adopted EVA (Economic Value Added) as a measure to maximize shareholder value.

EVA estimates how much value-added is created as a result of economic activity after various costs, such as the opportunity cost of equity capital, are paid. It was eventually linked to the compensation of all managers above the level of department heads. For a president of a "network company," the performance of his company determined 50% of his bonus. Twenty-five percent depended on Sony's overall performance, and the remaining 25% was determined by subjective goal management. Also, in the case of midlevel managers, performance of individual business units was weighted more in bonus calculations. Less weight was placed on Sony's overall performance and about 25% weight was placed on the performance of the network company. By contrast, lower-level employees' bonuses were determined almost entirely through interviews with their bosses. Bonuses were determined by relative evaluation by bosses, who used a curve with fixed percentages for each bracket. Some employees' bonuses could be low even if their company's performance was good.[11] Workers were not generally happy with this system.

EVA had some good effects. It induced managers to reduce investment and inventories significantly, and it facilitated business exit. For instance, EVA was a very effective measure to reduce inventory level. Each company tried to reduce inventory and implement effective SCM (supply chain management) to enhance the EVA, because inventory cost is calculated by multiplying inventories with weighted average capital cost. The inventory level went down to an average of 50 days stock in 2001, versus four to five months in the past.[12] It also made company presidents' performance transparent. But it was also more appropriate for some divisions, such as those that produced mature product lines, for which improving operational efficiency and resource allocation are important goals, than it was for determining whether to make a long-term investment or enter a new business. For instance, if a manager reduced his investment in R&D, his EVA could improve in the short run, but his business might suffer in the long run. Nonetheless, some company managers used EVA indiscriminately, even to evaluate proposals for a research development plan. Not surprisingly, long-term investments that had uncertain payoffs were discouraged,[13] and only projects with visible short-term outcomes were sponsored.

Under the company system, Sony also moved its employees in planning and product development from the group level to individual companies. At the group level, these personnel worked to develop radically new products for all of Sony. Because their new product development plans often required long-term investments, many of their projects were canceled by company managers. For instance, Sony's

VAIO computer was intended to revolutionize the personal computer by integrating it with audio and video functions. When its audacious purple-colored, ultra-light notebook with integrated audio and video functions was introduced, consumers regarded it as another "wow" product of Sony. As the division was under pressure to generate short-term profits, more resources were dedicated in developing products for the next quarter than in developing a next generation of innovative products. It was no wonder that VAIO became boring and another "me-too" product. Engineers, who joined the VAIO division to develop a revolutionary personal computer, became so demoralized that they did not even bother to attend its own exhibition of new products.[14] R&D was curtailed further when Sony's performance deteriorated sharply, and the need to improve cash flow was urgent. Company presidents saved on R&D costs by transferring researchers to production lines. In short, the company system provided managers the incentive to cut R&D spending to improve the bottom line, which in turn negatively affected Sony's long-term performance. As Figure 2.1 shows, both Sony's R&D investment and R&D in proportion to sales were cut after the company system was introduced in 1994.

In the past, under the principle of freedom and open-mindedness, Sony researchers pursued their own pet projects, which were not directly related to its main businesses, but often resulted in development of unique products. For instance, Kutaragi's passion for the game machine contributed to Sony's success with PlayStation. When company managers had to pay for R&D expenses out of their pockets under the company system, however, the immediate effect was to cut all projects that did not have immediate paybacks. It was no wonder that Sony had failed to come up with ingenious products since the 1990s.

Before Sony began using EVA, divisions shared technology and cooperated with each other. For instance, there was technological interdependence among the audio, TV, and VAIO divisions, and each assisted the others when asked. It was difficult to achieve such a cooperative relationship after EVA was introduced. If company number one asked company number two for assistance, company number two expected to be paid. Most managers of those companies, did not have much experience working from the perspective of the entire organization, and they used EVA both to evaluate R&D investments and to respond to other units' requests to share resources. According to Ando, "Company presidents were aggressive individuals but at the same time they were young and less experienced. Their thinking could be sometimes too much short-term-oriented." On other occasions, network companies did not delegate enough power to individual business unit managers.

Another consequence of having independent companies and short-term performance evaluation was that individual companies increased their investment in mature products, which could be milked for quick profits. The best example of this tendency was the "legacy problem," in which the lifespan of conventional analog products was extended and investment in new digital products was discouraged. This was the reason why Sony held on to its mature Trinitron CRT-based WEGA TV, and did not invest in flat panels such as PDPs or LCDs.

From the perspective of a company in charge of TVs, a huge CRT production facility remained an asset; the company should not prematurely exit a business that remained profitable. When Sony built its TV manufacturing plant in Pittsburgh, it presumed it would have 10 years to recoup this investment. The president in charge of TVs had no clear incentive to scrap this factory and make another huge new investment in LCD and PDP displays because that decision would have a direct impact on his bottom line. Nor did Sony HQ want to give up the immediate profits that WEGA generated because it needed to improve overall profitability and pay down the company's debt. In a sense, company presidents and Sony HQ had common interests and implicitly colluded with each other not to hurry investment on digital products.

Also, it was difficult for the CEO or HQ staff to interfere with individual companies' decisions, especially when they were making profits. Sony's audio and TV companies enjoyed big profits until earlier in this decade, and they felt no need to develop digital technology. Even if Idei had urged them to respond to this challenge, they would have ignored him. The TV business began responding only after it began suffering huge losses in 2003. Similarly, because Sony had been so successful in CDs, its audio company believed that MD would be a big hit as the next-generation CD. This division was profitable at that time with MD, and had no interest in looking for a substitute such as MP3 players. When MP3 players came to market, Sony responded with High MD, an improved version of MD. Later, when it introduced

MP3 players, it tried to use the ATRAC music file format from MDs. And so when Apple introduced iPod to the Japanese market, Sony's audio company could not respond, and finally gave up, just as Apple had said in its ad: "Goodbye, MD."

### Conflicts among Companies

An important trend in the digital revolution is convergence, so that products that used to be distinct begin to overlap and compete. In the analog world, TVs, audio, and computers were independent. As digitalization has accelerated, however, TV and DVDs can now be watched on a PC, and audio CDs can be played on a PC. Although this conflict may have been common to every electronics manufacturer, it was especially severe for Sony, given both its breadth of products and its nearly independent companies under the company structure.

In particular, after the ten companies were reorganized into three network companies, the units for performance evaluation were widened, and the connection between performance and rewards became vaguer. For example, the management goal of Home Networks was to create new value in home networks. In other words, any product or service that "Digital Dream Kids" used in the living room became this division's responsibility. The vagueness of this business concept caused much confusion, and different divisions came up with similar products that cannibalized each other.

For example, Idei wanted to develop a new TV concept in 2001. He created a company, named NTSC (Network Terminal Solution Company) within the Home Network Company. NTSC developed a product, called Cocoon, which could record TV programs automatically on a hard disk. This product had two tuners so that it was possible to watch one TV program while recording and storing another. Cocoon also introduced software that emulated the TV watching pattern of its users, analyzed viewers' TV program preferences, and recorded programs automatically. When the hard disc became full, Cocoon overwrote its old recordings. In order to develop this product, any TV-related technology belonged to the TV company, and the hard disk and software technology to record TV programs belonged to the VAIO company, and the DVD belonged to the video company. Some consumers wanted to keep recorded programs stored on hard disk using DVD, but DVD development was delayed. As a result, Cocoon was released without DVD capability and did not sell. Cocoon failed because the video company concentrated on developing its own product, and was lukewarm in supporting the DVD for Cocoon, which competed with its own product. Only later did an improved version of Cocoon (Sugoroku), which could record programs onto DVDs, become successful.

With its hard drive and DVD, the Sugoroku conflicted with PSX, which was a hybrid machine that combined PlayStation 2 with a DVD recording function. Sugoroku was launched by the Home Network Company, and PSX belonged to the Broadband Network Company, which ran the game business. With two products that had similar functionality, it was inevitable that Sony's marketing efforts were scattered, and consumers were confused as to which DVD player was Sony's major product. And when Sony slashed the price of PSX due to disappointing sales, the prices of Sony's similar products, including Sugoroku, had to be marked down.

Another conflict among business divisions broke out in digital music players. Sony had developed two products, Memory Stick Walkman, a portable music player, which could store music files on a memory stick, and a VAIO music clip, which had internal memory. In 1999, two years before Apple developed the iPod, these products were developed independently by Sony's audio and VAIO companies. Had these companies shared resources, they could have developed a better product. Because both products were inferior to the iPod, however, neither was successful. It is said that Idei ordered the VAIO division to develop a music player because the audio division did not show any interest in doing so.

Some years later, Sony had another chance to develop a digital audio player. It decided to merge a debt-ridden affiliate, Aiwa, which remained its subsidiary, and had Aiwa develop a new music player to compete against Apple's iPod. In 2003, Aiwa's project team developed a music player that stored music files in memory using a USB port and USB speakers. This product used the MP3 music compression format and USB port, both of which were industry standards. But Sony's Personal Audio Company rejected this effort, and instead tried to develop products using its own compression format, ATRAC, and its own recording media, MD. From the perspective of the Personal Audio Company, Aiwa was trying to undermine its effort by using the competitors' formats, albeit ones that were industry standards. Suddenly, when Aiwa's product development was almost done, its project was canceled by the order of Sony's Corporate Vice President Kutaragi, who was in charge of all electronics, game, and component businesses. The Aiwa project team was integrated into the Personal Audio Company only to be dissolved. Personal Audio Company, in a prime example of Sony's NIH syndrome, had influenced Kutaragi to make this decision.

### Separate Content Business

Sony's other businesses, such as music, movies, and financial services, were organized as completely separate organizations. Morita often insisted that "hardware and software are two wheels of the electronics business," but creating synergy between these two businesses was almost impossible.

Sony Music Entertainment and Sony Pictures Entertainment, subsidiaries of Sony America, were independent corporations. Supervision of these companies by Sony HQ was limited, and Sony's managers, who did not know much about the entertainment business, had to depend on local managers. The CEO of Sony America, Mickey Schulhof, tried to create synergies between hardware and software, but his efforts often backfired, especially when he tried to interfere with individual business units' management.[15] Vander Dussen, who was in charge of Sony America's electronics business, commented, "After the acquisition, Mickey was always pushing us to help make the pictures operation more successful but without taking any credit and at actual cost to ourselves. There has to be an honest and fair distribution of money on both sides, but that wasn't what was happening. For example, we might want to include a disc with a tape machine as a premium. Warner would cooperate with us and sell us the discs at a sizable discount. But, Mickey would insist that we pay list price to Columbia, and do all the work besides. I said, 'Fine, but let's recognize up front so that everyone knows that this will impact our profitability in a negative way.' In other words, we didn't want this to happen without recognition that we were bending over backward on behalf of the company as a whole. The next thing I know, Mickey turns around and complains to Ohga that we were not cooperating. There was constant, ongoing controversy rather than a spirit of cooperation."[16] Synergies could be created, but without proper incentives to each business they were impossible to achieve.

Sony's internal conflict between software and hardware businesses became an open secret in 1991, and the press began to issue reports. Sony's hardware executives complained that Sony's software people estranged outside suppliers of content that was necessary to the success of Data Discman. This antagonism became conspicuous when Sony announced the DAT (Digital Audiotape) Walkman. When it launched this product, Sony tried to release digital cassettes with music from Sony Music. Firms in the recording industry opposed the release of their sound sources on the DAT format because they feared piracy could become more prevalent if digital recording was available. Shulhof, Sony Music's CEO, sided with the recording industry on this issue, which clearly angered managers in Sony's hardware units.[17]

More generally, synergies between Sony's hardware and content businesses were increasingly difficult to achieve during the era of digital convergence because these businesses had competing interests that had not existed in the analog era. When recording was physical (such as a vinyl record or a CD), hardware and software were complementary. For example, when recording media changed from vinyl to CD, it worked for Sony to have a content company. As Sony released its own music content on CD, consumers enjoyed excellent sound quality and migrated to CD. For a hardware company, it was also advantageous to promote CDs, because it could make money by manufacturing both CDs and CD players. When it became possible to share music files over networks, however, consumers who formerly bought Sony music CDs could now illegally download music files for free. Yet it was in the interests of Sony's hardware business to help consumers download content easily in order to increase its hardware sales. Therefore, when Sony made digital music players such as the Memory Stick Walkman and the VAIO Music Clip, Sony Music opposed their release because it feared that illegal downloads for digital music players would affect their business negatively. According to a high-ranking executive at Sony, "An internal content business is not necessarily an asset but it can also be a liability since we need to protect the interests of the content business. We could have never done like Steve Jobs did with iPod. In my view, he gave away content too cheaply." Further, Sony tended to respect and follow Sony Music's opinion rather than force it to follow orders, even after Schulhof was fired and Sony regained control over its U.S. subsidiary. This incident may also reflect Japanese companies' bias to favor consensus over open confrontation, as well as Sony's principle of inducing voluntary cooperation instead of coercing it.

Sony's content divisions remained cool to Idei's suggestion that they should keep up with technological innovation in hardware to create synergy. Sony founded Sony Broadband Entertainment, Inc. to create synergy between hardware and software in 2000, and explored ways to exploit Sony's digital assets. It also tried to develop game content with Sony Pictures Digital Entertainment (SPDE). Sony founded Network Application and Content Service Sector (NACS) in April 2002, and appointed Yuki Nozoe, a veteran of Sony Pictures, as president and charged him to create synergy and convergence between hardware and content. NACS researched interfaces between content and hardware to develop music management software similar to Apple's iTunes, but made little progress because of frequent reorganizations and the music business's opposition. In 2004, Sony set up the Connect Company to develop music management software and allow Mora to sell music files over the Internet. Sony's hardware side and Sony Music each appointed managers to become co-presidents of Connect Company, but they could not agree on anything, and the resultant Connect Player was riddled with technical problems. After this project failed, the two co-presidents left the company.[18]

Some critics doubt whether Sony could ever create synergy between its electronics and content businesses. According to an analyst at Goldman Sachs, "Sony has two DNAs, its two founders, Ibuka and Morita. Ibuka was an engineer and enjoyed playing with technology. Morita, although an engineer himself, was a born entrepreneur. Morita was from a rich family. By his nature, he was interested in making toys for adults. That explains partly why he entered the entertainment business. Even when Ibuka was struggling to develop a Trinitron CRT and incurring huge losses, Morita was constructing a fancy Ginza building. In a sense, both enjoyed their own hobbies, and these two DNAs never mixed. Perhaps, Morita had a very naïve idea of synergy, that it would be naturally created if he put these two businesses together, which never happened. I know that there are some people out there arguing that a synergy is illusory. Apple's iPod, however, clearly demonstrates that there is indeed a synergy, but it can be created without owning them."

## Absence of HQ's Control Function

Although structural problems and conflicting incentives made it hard for Sony to create synergies among its disparate units, various mechanisms might have prevented individual business units from becoming silos. Sony's CEO and corporate staff could have promoted resource sharing and cooperation among companies. Most diversified enterprises that adopt the multidivisional structure have corporate staff that supervise the performance of individual business units and make strategic decisions from a corporate perspective.[19] In the past, the independence of Sony's business units under its business group system and its corporate culture had not caused big problems, partly because of the charismatic leadership of Morita, Ibuka, and Ohga. These men could influence business unit heads just by asking questions or by presenting their own ideas. A hint from the founders was enough to make business heads feel they should at least be open to communications with other business unit heads and cooperate with them to develop new products.

Idei did not, however, have such influence. He delegated power and responsibility based on Western organizational principles, and he typically declined to intervene in decision making at the company level. As a company transitions from a charismatic founder to an administratively-oriented CEO, however, the downsides of a company system become evident.

Nonetheless, Idei might have built a strong corporate staff that would provide Sony's HQ a reason to push the firm's companies to share resources and cooperate. Idei defined the role of Sony Group's HQ as an "active investor," which was to maximize shareholder value, and defined the role of the board of directors as only supervisory. Sony's HQ had a minimal role and had no power to induce resource sharing and cooperation. Instead, Idei included company presidents on the group headquarters' management committee and hoped they would voluntarily cooperate with each other. As a consequence, Group HQ's role as an "active investor" did not go beyond financial control.

There had also been a general planning department in Sony HQ that developed strategy and new businesses. As a staff organization, however, it could not force individual companies to act. In its 2001 reorganization, Sony abolished the "strategic planning function" from this department, further stripping it of power, and instead encouraged "strategic alliances" between business divisions. According to Idei, "We also embarked on a review of the corporate organization, in particular the traditional pyramid model, and management systems, namely the command-and-control–based systems. In doing so, we decided to create a network-based organizational structure. Specifically, the transfer of a wide scope of authority will promote the autonomous management of each business and facilitate swifter decision-making. At the same time, under the leadership of the Sony Group Headquarters, we will bolster strategic alliances among the five pillars and formulate integrated group-wide strategies with the view to maximizing corporate value. We call this new management model 'integrated/decentralized management.'"[20]

Under this principle, Sony set up a Global Hub and Electronics HQ to foster voluntary strategic alliances. Network organization through voluntary cooperation was theoretically possible, but hard to achieve. As the Cocoon example illustrated, if a new product was to be developed by "voluntary" alliances among several independent business units, this development would be delayed. Nor could "voluntary" alliances prevent independent companies from competing with each other with similar products, as happened with Memory Stick Walkman and VAIO Music Clip. It was almost impossible to expect voluntary alliances between hardware and content businesses, which were separate organizations and had distinct interests. Sony's corporate-level organization and strategy dramatically contrast with those of Samsung Electronics, where the group-level staff exercises strong coordination.

In addition, Idei did not spend enough time coordinating Sony's independent companies. He had too many duties inside and outside Sony to perform all of his obligations effectively.[21] He became an outside director of GM and Nestlé, and a chairman of the Japanese Government's IT Strategy Advising Committee. To take only one example of Idei's leadership, there was much disagreement among Sony executives about whether Sony should enter the S-LCD joint venture with Samsung Electronics. In order to calm down the internal dissent over this joint venture, Sony's Corporate Vice President Kutaragi had to ask Idei to summon every executive officer to the opening ceremony of this venture so that these individuals would not raise any dispute in the future. This shows how long it took to achieve consensus within Sony. At Samsung Electronics, no one would have dared raise a protest about a project that the Office of Secretaries had examined and that Chairman Lee had approved. Once Samsung's executives got an order, they ran to accomplish the mission.

In 2003, Sony announced a restructuring plan, "Transformation 60," which was intended to raise operating profitability to 10% by 2006, Sony's 60th anniversary. The plan laid out five goals for Sony: (1) to concentrate on strategic business; (2) to restructure its global production activity; (3) to simplify management, sales, and marketing; (4) to reform design processes, quality management, and purchasing; and (5) to reinforce its sourcing strategy. Sony proposed to reduce its headcount by 20,000 staff. Previously, Sony had announced in 1999 that it would reduce the number of manufacturing facilities from 70 to 52, but it could not carry out that restructuring plan. It closed a few factories and reduced headcount slightly, but no one had taken responsibility for implementing this plan. Sony's failed restructuring effort contrasts with that of Samsung Electronics, when it cut more than 30% of its workforce and closed 52 product lines during the Asian financial crisis.

Sony's frequent reorganizations have caused some of its problems. Although it is sometimes necessary to reorganize in order to respond to market changes, managers do not have enough time to improve performance when firms restructure too frequently. Strategy becomes inconsistent, and employees quickly become dispirited. For example, Idei founded Digital Network Service (DNS), as a corporate staff organization in 1999 to develop a set-top box for digital broadcasting and software for distributing digital content. Because DNS was a staff organization, it had to persuade Sony's line companies to collaborate. Faced with this limitation, DNS was quickly absorbed into the Broadcasting Company, which manufactured and sold hardware for broadcasting, and was then later integrated into the Communication System Solution Network Company (CSNC). After 15 months, however, another reorganization occurred, and CSNC was consolidated into the Broadband Network Center (BNC) and Communication Service Company (CSC). Most of the DNS business was taken over by CSC, but some went to BNC. DNS's original core members were scattered into other organizations. New managers in charge of new organizations often cancelled development projects that their predecessors had pursued. Many times they did so simply because they were not interested in the project or misunderstood its value. Frequent reorganization provides managers with the wrong incentive to pursue projects with visible short-term outcomes and to give up long-term investments because it is uncertain whether such expenditures will be supported after the next reorganization.[22] These problems occurred throughout Sony.

## Corporate Culture and Organizational Structure of Samsung Electronics

### Corporate Culture of Samsung Electronics

When he founded Samsung Group, Byung-chull Lee laid out three missions: (1) contribute to his nation's economic development, (2) pursue economic rationality, and (3) value human resources. Such missions reflected Korea's economic situation at the time of Samsung Group's founding, when there was little social infrastructure and human resources were in short supply. Samsung's corporate culture emphasizes integration and efficiency with talented employees. In order to reduce the costs associated with trial and error and to take advantage of employees' experience, Samsung desired competent workers. Since its founding, Samsung has accumulated know-how to improve efficiency and has learned how to systematize this knowledge and spread it quickly throughout the entire organization.[23]

As an affiliate of the Samsung Group, Samsung Electronics has shared Samsung Group's corporate culture and management techniques. A unique aspect of Samsung Electronics' corporate culture, beyond what it shares with Samsung Group, has been its execution-oriented culture. For instance, it constructed its first semiconductor plant in only six months, as opposed to the industry norm of two or three years. In another instance, Samsung workers were about to move fragile semiconductor manufacturing equipment. Only that morning, however, the factory's employees realized that the road to the factory needed to be paved to prevent the manufacturing equipment from being damaged. So they paved the road in a couple of hours while using fans to dry the pavement.[24]

Another important element of Samsung Group's corporate culture is loyalty, with an emphasis on integrity and can-do spirit. Samsung Group has emphasized integrity and corporate ethics, prohibiting bribe taking or personal profiteering, and has implemented ways to educate both new recruits and incumbent workers. It has also implemented a meticulous auditing system to ensure that unethical practices do not take place. Auditors monitor workers closely and punish offenders. Samsung's employees are proud of the firm's clean corporate culture. Samsung even prepares various scenarios of bribery cases and lets employees discuss and decide on solutions during training.[25] Samsung's notion of unethical behaviors is, however, restricted to taking bribes or personal profiteering from inside information. This is a different matter from that of emphasizing social responsibility and law-abiding behavior. As long as bribery to politicians or government officials would benefit the company, Samsung did not hesitate doing so, as publicized in the recent scandal.[26]

In their loyalty to the company, Samsung employees can be like bees, which often sacrifice themselves for their kingdom. When the Fair Trade Commission tried to investigate illegal internal transactions, an employee tried to destroy evidence by reformatting his PC's hard drive, knowing that he might be punished. Samsung implicitly encourages this kind of loyalty and self-sacrifice, even though these actions may be unethical and illegal. Samsung Electronics' employees are also highly disciplined, and try to achieve their missions, however difficult they might be.

At the same time, there has always been tension within the organization. Samsung Electronics' own internal audit team and Samsung Group's audit team both have the power to dismiss anyone immediately. In general, Samsung Electronics' managers fear the finance/accounting, auditing, and HR teams of the Group's Office of Secretaries. This fear has maintained loyalty and integrity within the organization.

Samsung Electronics has maintained its organizational structure and corporate culture by recruiting workers who can adapt to its culture and are disciplined enough to endure hardship. New recruits are trained for 27 days. Most training has focused on shaping their state of mind when they work, and the remaining training has focused on the individual companies they will work in. Recruits who do not seem to fit in have been asked to leave. Whenever an employee has been promoted, he has had to go through training similar to that of his cohorts. Even for managers, much of the training emphasizes loyalty and a can-do spirit.

Samsung's founding principle of emphasizing economic rationality and efficiency has also influenced the results-oriented culture. Employees believe that the businesses in which Samsung operates should be the best in the world, and they always think of ways to achieve this goal. In 1993, Byung-chull Lee commented, "There are only three ways to compete. The first is who is the cheapest among all competitors that can make the same product; the second is whose quality is the highest if the price level is about the same; the third is who is the earliest [in getting to market] if every other condition is the same." The founder's values have been etched in Samsung employees minds, and they constantly follow three precepts: "we cannot lose but win," "we have to do our job the best we can," and "we have to accomplish our tasks completely." In this way, Samsung' corporate culture has mixed the founder's entrepreneurship and performance orientation with the "hungry spirit" and "can-do spirit" of Korea during its developmental stage.[27]

## GBM Structure

Samsung Electronics has maintained a strong business division structure, similar to Sony's old "business group structure," which consists of business units managed independently by business unit managers. Unlike Sony's "company structure," business units in Samsung Electronics do not have their own balance sheets and income statements. Samsung Electronics consists of Global Business Managers (GBM) that organize the firm along major product divisions. Prior to 1998, Samsung Electronics also had product divisions focused mainly on production and domestic sales. R&D and overseas sales were managed separately.

When Chairman Lee initiated the "New Management Movement," there was some emphasis on localization; the regional HQ system was implemented, and production complexes were built worldwide. After realizing the limitations of this system, Samsung moved back to its global structure. The implementation of this structure has not changed much since Samsung Electronics adopted it.

Samsung's GBM organization is a global product division organization, divided by major businesses. Business division heads are responsible for production, sales, and personnel within their respective divisions. As of 2006, Samsung Electronics had five broadly defined sectors: Digital Media, Telecommunications, Digital Appliances, Semiconductors, and LCDs. Within these sectors are 13 GBMs, which are more narrowly defined product lines, such as computers, printing images, mobile communications, and so forth (see Figure 6.4). Based in Korea, the GBMs are in charge of production and sales for their businesses. They are responsible for profitability; decide strategy, technical support, pricing, transfer prices, and output levels; and manage foreign subsidiaries. These powers allow them to make decisions and implement initiatives quickly. In order to supplement the GBM structure's insular orientation, Samsung Electronics also runs several cross-business team organizations, such as the Digital Solution Team, which develops digital convergence products or network products.

Under the GBM structure, Samsung Electronics has offered very generous remuneration to its employees. For example, Samsung Electronics has based employees' bonuses on the financial performance of their divisions. Employees have received cash bonuses as part of a profit sharing (PS) scheme, which distributes profits that exceed a target level among all employees according to the performance of their divisions, of up to 50% of their annual salaries; in 2006, the average bonus was about 11% of annual salary.[28] In addition, Samsung Electronics pays a productivity incentive (PI), which factors in a combination of evaluations for the department, its business, and the company as a whole. These bonuses can be up to 300% of an employee's annual base payment.[29] Again, there exists a wide variance of PIs across business divisions.

Notably, Samsung Electronics has used EVA, cash flow, and earnings per share to calculate bonuses, the same measures Sony has used to evaluate individual companies' performance. In this regard, both Samsung Electronics and Sony have emphasized short-term performance. Samsung Electronics has operated closer to the principle of a multidivisional structure, however, in that it has paid incentives to its employees according to their department's and business division's performance.

*Figure 6.4* Samsung Electronics' Organizational Structure

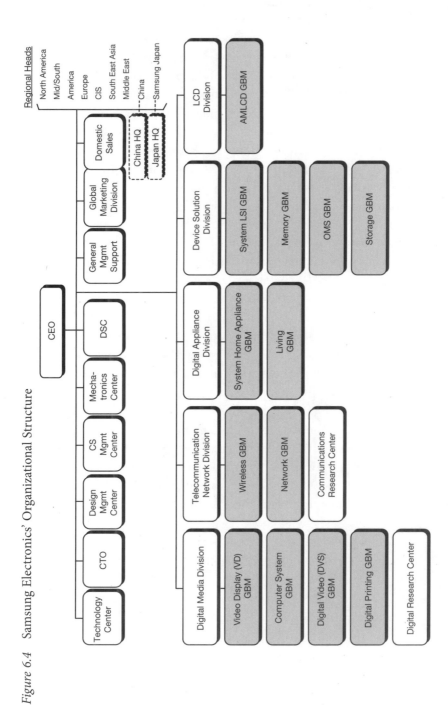

The financial incentives for Sony's employees have been weaker because these bonuses were determined on a curve; a Sony employee can receive a low bonus even though his business had a great year. At Samsung Electronics, however, the variable portion of employees' annual compensation has sometimes been higher than the fixed portion is. In this respect, Samsung Electronics is managed more like U.S. firms, which often pay large financial incentives to their employees. Samsung Electronics is unusual in Korea, where most firms emphasize equity over performance. It is not clear whether Samsung Electronics can avoid keeping its business divisions from becoming silos so long as it provides strong financial incentives based on short-term performance. In this way, Samsung Electronics may discourage long-term investment and interdivisional cooperation.

### Office of Secretaries

The greatest difference in the organizational structure between Samsung Electronics and Sony is that the former is controlled by an Office of Secretaries. The "Office of Secretaries" is an old name, used by the founder. Its name as of 2007 is "Group Strategic Planning Office," but many insiders and outsiders still call it by its original name.[30] It is a group-level staff organization that helps the Chairman of Samsung Group oversee individual affiliates. Its core functions include finance/accounting, auditing, planning, public relations, and human resource management, including the hiring/firing of all executives within Samsung Group. All important strategic decisions and sizable investment decisions, even at the individual affiliate level, have to be reviewed by this Office. In other words, all of Samsung Electronics' important decisions are made by Chairman Lee with the assistance of this Office.

Chairman Kun-hee Lee officially discussed the Office of Secretaries' role when he became Samsung Group's Chairman in 1987. "The former chairman made 80% of decisions, the Office of Secretaries 10%, and presidents of individual affiliates only 10% in the past. From now on, I am going to change to a system in which the chairman will make 20%, the Office of Secretaries 40%, and affiliate presidents 40%."[31] In this regard, the official CEO of Samsung Electronics, Jong-yong Yun, is not a true CEO, as this term is used to describe top executives in Western firms. He cannot sign off on major investment decisions and cannot hire or fire his own executives. Yun is more accurately classified as a COO, because he makes only 40% of the decisions pertaining to his firm and is supervised by Chairman Lee and the Office of Secretaries. In other words, the only true CEO within Samsung Group is Mr. Lee. Yun focuses on daily decisions related to Samsung Electronics and is its official representative.

The Office of Secretaries runs the group as a whole and develops its future growth strategy, including business entry and exit. Although Samsung Electronics' GBM business structure consists of independently run businesses, the finance department of Samsung Electronics and the finance team of the Office of Secretaries can monitor these businesses' performance daily on a real-time basis. Samsung was early to invest heavily in information systems such as ERP, which has allowed it to monitor the performance of each business unit in any location on a real-time basis. Managers in charge of GBM may be given full authority and decision-making power, but they cannot relax because they know they are being closely watched.

One peculiarity of Samsung Electronics' organization is that the personnel function is under the CFO rather than the CEO. Do-seok Choi is Samsung Electronics' CFO. Officially, he reports to Jong-yong Yun, and he sometimes takes order from Yun. These orders are, however, only for narrowly defined business issues.[32] For example, when Samsung Electronics needs to make an important investment decision, the related business unit writes a proposal, which is reviewed by Samsung Electronics' finance department. After Choi reports the proposal to Yun, it is passed to the finance team of the Office of Secretaries, and it is approved by the Chief of Office of Secretaries, Hak-soo Lee. Approval by the Office of Secretaries means that the Chairman of Group approves the project. Similarly, Yun can give his input on appointing/dismissing executives, but Chairman Lee has the final say. Figure 6.5 is a sketch of Samsung Electronics' real, but unofficial, organizational structure.

Samsung Electronics and other affiliates of the Samsung Group have been able to share resources and to create synergies, because of interventions by the Office of Secretaries. When there are conflicts between several businesses and cooperation among them is required, the Office of Secretaries steps in and coordinates. Business units have to accept its resolutions, which may prove that it is possible to create

*Figure 6.5* Relations among Key Executives at Samsung Electronics

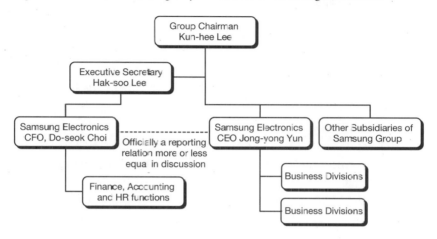

synergies via involuntary cooperation or fiat. In contrast, Sony's policy of "integrated decentralization" tried to create synergy by voluntary "strategic alliance" among businesses, but success was limited.

## The Problem of Samsung Electronics' Organizational Structure

### Severe Internal Competition

Samsung Electronics has several potential problems. First, there is severe competition among internal business units. Samsung Electronics GBMs can become silos just as Sony's independent companies did. Among Samsung Electronics' major GBMs, competition between the memory, mobile communication, and LCD businesses is severe; cooperation often does not happen voluntarily; and conflicts about products and transfer prices are frequent. For example, a unit that manufactures MP3 players complains that Samsung's memory division sells flash memory to Apple too cheaply. Samsung's LCD business produces LCD panels and Samsung SDI, another Samsung affiliate produces PDP panels. Both supply to Samsung's TV manufacturing business, and compete fiercely with each other. The computer business's PDA has competed with another PDA made by the mobile communication business. Likewise, heads of the GBMs compete fiercely with each other to demonstrate their units' achievements.

In one incident, President Sang-wan Lee who is in charge of LCDs, announced the development of the world's largest LCD TV. The next day, President Kee-tai Lee of mobile telecommunications announced the development of a three million pixel digital camera phone. Hereupon, Chang-gyu Hwang of the semiconductor business held a press conference to announce the development of the world's first 8G flash memory. In fact, Samsung encourages such tense internal competition. At a dinner after a golf outing with executives, CEO Yun donated an expensive driver as a prize to the team that pledged to drink the most "atomic shots," beer spiked with whiskey. The bidding went up to 10 shots, and everyone thought that was the outer limit. The team headed by President Dae-je Chin of the Digital Media Division surprised everyone by bidding 15 and downing them. Chin and his team simply hated to lose.[33]

Yet one of the likely reasons for Samsung Electronics' success has been the tradition of mutual assistance. For example, when the memory business experienced huge losses, it could not have survived without support from the home appliances and telecommunication businesses. Even now, internal exchanges are frequent. For instance, both the LCD business and the mobile telecommunication business get supplies from the semiconductor business, and internal buyers get the highest priority when there is a supply shortage.

These businesses also need to collaborate when they develop new products that involve the design of new parts and components.[34] In the future, Samsung Electronics must find ways to ensure cooperation and resource sharing among competitive business units. Although the Office of Secretaries can intervene on visible projects or problems, it cannot deal with every minor issue. The biggest potential problem of Samsung's organization is that the idea of the zero-sum game, in which one side's win is the other side's loss, may become prevalent among managers. If these managers cannot see ways to create win-win solutions, it will be difficult to create synergies internally, as well as through strategic alliances with and acquisitions of foreign firms. Samsung's past failures in technology-sourcing strategic alliances and acquisitions firms may in part reflect the widespread competitive mentality of its employees.

### Organizational Fatigue

Another problem at Samsung Electronics is organizational fatigue. Because employees are constantly monitored and are under great pressure to achieve difficult goals, they become burned out. Further, they know they can be fired at any time. Samsung Electronics' suppliers, some of which are other Samsung Group affiliates, feel similar pressure because Samsung demands tight delivery, and it frequently slashes the prices it pays for supplies.

Some foreign observers call the management style of Samsung "fear-based management." Samsung employees are very loyal to the firm when they are working there. If they leave the company against their will, however, their anger toward it can cancel out their old loyalty. Samsung's corporate culture and organization may have been effective tools when Samsung was a follower that had to catch up with market leaders by reducing costs through mass production, but they may now constrain Samsung from being a creative leader.

Samsung Electronics, as a late entrant, has tried to maintain a willingness to learn from others. As it enjoys good performance and is acknowledged as an industry leader, however, it shows some hints of hubris. It may become less inclined to correct its internal problems. Also, as Samsung Electronics becomes larger and hires a wider variety of people, employees' loyalty may become weaker than it was. There have already been several cases in which Samsung Electronics employees have tried to sell proprietary technologies to Samsung's competitors. Maintaining its strong loyalty and organizational discipline, which have been crucial to its remarkable growth, will be one of Samsung Electronics' biggest challenges.

# 7

# From Founders
# to Professional Managers

I knew that running Sony was impossible because it was a company driven by the founders' vision: the founders' personal vision was the basis and the standard for every decision.... Normally, there is a clear line between the owners of a company and professional managers, but in our organization that separation never occurred. Ohga is not an owner, but he behaves as if he were. His logic is theirs. And Sony logic until now has been based on personal relationships, on friendships, and that produces phenomena like Mickey [Schulhof], a second tier of ownership. Sony is an extraordinary company in many respects, but one of them is certainly that we have grown to half a hundred billion dollars on the founders' logic. Now we need professional managers.

*– Nobuyuki Idei, former CEO of Sony*[1]

The company [Samsung Electronics] is majority held by foreign shareholders now, but it is still run as a family concern.

*—Devan Koo, Aberdeen Asset Management, Singapore*[2]

Although the organizing principles for Sony and Samsung were based on decentralization and delegation, the outcomes have been quite different. The biggest difference between the two firms' organization structures is that in Samsung, the Office of Secretaries has managed the individual companies and assisted Chairman Lee by promoting cooperation among the affiliates and evaluating the performance of division heads. In Sony, the individual business units, called companies, had too much autonomy, which undermined the ability of the CEOs to execute strategy. This difference may be attributable to distinct CEOs' leadership styles and corporate governance structures. Now it is time to examine the status and leadership of Sony and Samsung Electronics' CEOs more closely and to discuss these firms' problems in more depth.

Idei was the first salary-man to become CEO of Sony. His biggest challenge was how to follow the charismatic leaders of Sony's founder generation. When Sony's performance declined, Idei's leadership was questioned, and his power as CEO was inevitably undermined by intra-organizational opposition.

Samsung Electronics has faced an entirely different problem. Chairman Lee is effectively the emperor of all Samsung Group's subsidiaries. The concern for Samsung Electronics is whether it will be an asset or a liability to have "an almighty CEO and his family continue ruling." Samsung Electronics must also avoid the difficulties that Sony experienced as it made the transition from the founder's generation to professional management.

## Sony's CEO and Governing Structure

### Founders and the Inner Circle

To understand Sony, you have to understand its founders, Ibuka and Morita. They were the catalysts behind Sony's ability to come up consistently with new products and to grow so quickly. Both have been revered by people within and outside Sony. Ibuka was an engineering genius, and Morita was an extraordinary manager. Ibuka led the development of many new products that Sony presented, and he fostered excellent engineers. Morita took charge of management, ventured into overseas markets, and led Sony's global enterprise. Both men were almighty, God-like figures in Sony, and no one ever dared go against them. They made decisions instantaneously—such as Morita's decision to develop the Walkman—which worked well when Sony was still a small rapidly-growing company. Even after Sony grew far larger, the company's decision-making structure did not change. When Sony's Morita decided to enter the film and music business, he did not ask for anyone's opinion before making this acquisition, nor did anyone dare to raise questions, even after it turned out disastrously.

Morita and Ibuka also formed many inner circles based on their personal relationships. Ohga, the next chairman, met Ibuka and Morita when Sony was still young. Ibuka and Morita thought highly of him and asked him to join Sony. Ohga, who had planned to be a professional singer, eventually became a manager in Sony and acted as if he were a founder as well, although he was not. He advised Sony on its recorder from the user's perspective.

Ogha's behavior and decision-making patterns were similar to those of Ibuka and Morita. In the early 1990s, when Sony was developing PlayStation, many inside Sony opposed this foray into the game business. Offended by Nintendo's walking away from the joint development of a machine that used the CD-ROM, however, Ohga pushed Sony to pursue the game business on its own, ignoring all objections. He often said, that "Ibuka contributed to Sony with the Trinitron TV, Morita with the Walkman, and me with the PlayStation." His management style was autocratic, and people describe his tenure as president and chairman as "the tyranny of Ohga."[3]

Other senior managers of Sony were also personal friends of Ibuka or Morita. Idei had known Ibuka well since his childhood, because he went to school with Ibuka's daughter. When Idei was stationed in France, he maintained his relationship with Morita's family by talking care of Morita's children, who were studying in Europe.

Before Morita was hospitalized by a stroke, he told Ohga to find his successor among engineers. Mrs. Morita, however, later told her husband, as he lay in bed, that Ohga was having trouble in finding an engineer for the next president, and she asked whether he might consider non-engineers. He gave his permission. This action made it possible for Idei to get the top job.[4] President Ando, appointed by Idei, was one of Morita's personal assistants. Schulhof, who became the CEO of Sony America, and Schmuckli, who represented Sony Europe, were also personally selected by Morita and were treated like family members, joining the inner circle.[5]

   Loyalty and commitment were expected from members of the inner circle, and some exercised strong power while manipulating their personal relationships with Sony's founders. Schulhof, for instance, acted as if he had founded Sony. Ohga and he both had pilot licenses, and became friends while using Sony's corporate planes as if they were their own. Schulhof was especially favored by Ohga; his nickname was "Ohga's son." He made decisions by directly communicating with Morita and Ohga by phone instead of going through official reporting channels, bypassing executives who had been dispatched from Sony HQ as his superiors.[6] He even ignored Morita's younger brother Masaki Morita, after he was made Sony America's Chairman, He became almost entirely uncontrollable as Akio Morita fell sick and Chairman Ohga took office; only when Idei was appointed as the new president was Schulhof dismissed.

### Idei and Board Reform

Chairman Idei joined Sony in 1960, right after he graduated from college. He began his career in Sony's International Sales Department, and spent much of his career in overseas sales. He played an important role in setting up and running Sony's European operation. From 1984 to 1986, he tried and failed to develop multimedia computers as the head of Sony's Micro Computer Division. Nor did he achieve much as the head of the Home Video Division in 1988. In 1989, Idei became an executive in charge of promotion, and managed international sales until he was selected as president by Ohga in 1994. Idei was well aware of the difficulty he faced when he was appointed president. Rather than being systematically managed, Sony still relied on the founders' decisions and personal judgments, just as it had when it was still a small family business.

   Soon after becoming president, Idei implemented the Company Structure—for two reasons. First, because of Sony's investments in music and entertainment, as well as overseas factories and real estate investments, in the late 1980s and early 1990s, it was deeply in debt and in poor financial health. Idei believed Sony would become more profitable if its individual business units had more autonomy. Second, he believed he could not run the company through personal charisma, as the founders had, and thought the new structure would make it easier to manage all of Sony.

Idei also reformed Sony's board in order to reinforce the headquarters' supervisory control over subsidiaries such as Sony America.[7] To do this, in 1997 Idei adopted a Western-style governance structure with outside directors. He believed that "in order to maintain a huge conglomerate with 5.6 trillion yen sales, the board must make decisions with the entire organization in mind rather than with a parochial perspective. For this to happen, meticulous discussions and examination by the board are indispensable, and the number of directors who can actually join this intense discussion should be limited to ten."[8]

Although Japanese commercial law endowed directors with executive power and supervisory rights, Sony divided the roles of executive officers from those of board directors. As a result, Sony Group's board, which had previously included 38 executives, was reduced to 10, including seven senior officers (the lowest position being the corporate vice president) and three outside directors: Peter Peterson, who had been the economic advisor to the president for the Nixon Administration, and was the chairman of Blackstone Group; Kenichi Suematsu, the chairman of Sakura Bank; and Hideo Ishihara of Goldman Sachs.

Over time, additional outside directors were included such as Goran Lindahl of ABB and Carlos Ghosn of Nissan. In 2003, Sony implemented an outside directors system, based on committees. It created the Nomination, Audit, and Compensation Committees. By this time, outside directors made up more than half the board and possessed considerable power.[9] For instance, an outside director was chairman of the board, and he could select what topics the board discussed.

## Problems with Sony's Governing Structure

### Succession and Leadership

When Idei was nominated president, he was the youngest of all the candidates. Chairman Ohga described the process of selecting Idei as "the elimination method" because all the other internal candidates had been eliminated one by one, and Idei was the only one left. Other executives and board members who were older and more experienced than Idei were unhappy about the nomination. In their opinion, Idei's performance had not been strong. He was not an engineer nor did he have charisma. Senior executives who had expected to become the new president either retired or moved to subsidiaries. They did not outwardly revolt against Idei, but they were not friendly. Moreover, former executive board members who were no longer on the board because of Idei's reform efforts were angry at him for taking away their power. To quiet them, Ohga sent personal letters, guaranteeing that although they were no longer board members, they still held all the privileges they used to enjoy.[10]

Beyond restructuring Sony to alleviate its financial troubles, Idei tried to develop new businesses with his network strategy, but his vision did not bring about any visible successes.[11] Because Idei knew relatively little about the electronics business and engineers did not have much faith in him, he lacked a base of support in the electronics sector. These engineers, who had been among Sony's power elite during the analog era, felt alienated as Idei emphasized the network, services, and entertainment rather than the conventional consumer electronics business.

Most Sony personnel had spent their careers developing analog products and were strongly attached to the analog products, such as Walkman, Trinitron TVs, CDs, and MiniDiscs, that had brought Sony glory in the past. Their technical expertise was in analog technologies such as circuit design, materials engineering, and mechanical engineering; they did not have much interest in or knowledge of digital technologies. Instead of actively revolting against Idei's digital and network strategies, however, they passively resisted.[12] They looked upon Idei as if he were advocating the New Economy during the IT bubble, and felt humiliated as if they were no longer useful. When the IT bubble burst in 2001 and Idei's vision had not materialized into any visible achievements, they began to criticize him more openly for destroying Sony's consumer electronics business. And then, as Sony's performance began spiraling downhill in 2003, those who had built their careers in the analog business and/or had been pushed out of power began to voice strong doubts about Idei's vision, strategies, and management capabilities. Ohga openly ignored Idei and expressed his dissatisfaction, frequently saying that "choosing Idei was a mistake." Chairman Idei no longer had credibility among employees.

Idei's leadership was the fundamental cause of Sony's deteriorating performance. Because Sony's governance structure emphasized freedom and open-mindedness and fostered the creativity and initiatives of individual business divisions, the entire organization could easily fall into chaos if its leadership was not strong enough to integrate its disparate parts.

With their charisma and association with Sony's founding years, Ibuka, Morita, and Ohga could exercise such leadership; Idei could not. He was more of an administrative manager who delegated decisions to divisional managers and controlled them through financial measures. Idei had other handicaps: his relatively young age and his tendency not to drive people out by force. Sony's problems were caused by the inconsistency between leadership and corporate culture. According to a high-level Sony executive, "Idei had inherited a strong power from his predecessors. He could have exercised it to move people into the direction he wanted to take. For any reason, he did not exercise his power at all or at least used it very inconsistently. That made subordinates question whether he would support them when in trouble. Slowly, they lost confidence in him and stopped listening to him."

Idei was also handicapped by a rocky succession process. While Morita was ill, Sony had no functioning CEO because its employees believed Morita would recover soon. When Ohga became CEO, there was no one to check his decisions. Further, Ohga failed to identify and mentor his successor. He began to look for a new president only when he approached his mandatory retirement age and selected Idei only because he had rejected everyone else.

Idei was not adequately trained to be CEO. At GE, by contrast, Jack Welch selected three candidates as his possible successor several years before his retirement, and prepared them for the CEO's job, making them compete in a "horse race" and evaluating them. When Jeff Immelt was at last nominated as his successor, Immelt was thoroughly prepared to conduct his duties as CEO.

Ohga remained Sony's honorary chairman after his retirement and interfered in Sony's businesses. He publicly criticized Idei's performance. These problems were typical of Japanese firms in which professional managers were taking the leadership reins from founders and owners.

## Internal Politics

Idei may have attempted to reform Sony's board in order to create a governance structure similar to that of Western firms. It is also possible that he wished to nullify the power base of incumbent executives and to dominate important decision-making processes with the support of a small number of executives and outside directors that he had appointed. In fact, Idei did control the board through this reform, and began to unfold his network strategy under the catchphrase of "Digital Dream Kids." In 2000, he nominated Ando as the president, and he himself became the CEO. As the honorary chairman, Ohga was pushed further away from the center of power.

When Sony's performance deteriorated, those who criticized Idei most forcefully were Ohga and Corporate Vice President Kutaragi, who had led the success of PlayStation. Kutaragi felt grateful to Ohga for supporting his efforts to develop PlayStation despite internal opposition, and Ohga was proud of him in return. Due to PlayStation's extraordinary success, Kutaragi became an executive board member of Sony at the age of 50 in 2000, which was considered rather young in Japan, and was appointed the corporate vice president in 2003. A strong character, Kutaragi was different from other Sony managers. As the title of the book about him, *The Maverick of Sony*, implies, Kutaragi often ignored the traditional hierarchy, had little consideration for his superiors and openly criticized them, and was infamous for his swift decisions and autocratic management style. In nominating Kutaragi as

Norio Ohga (left), holding a MiniDisc, and Ken Kutaragi (right), holding a new PlayStation 3. Photographs by Associated Press.

the corporate vice president in 2003, Idei had him take charge of games, consumer electronics, and the semiconductor businesses because he believed Kutaragi could create synergies among these areas. Sony was also developing PlayStation 3 at that time and had already invested substantially in a powerful new microprocessor called Cell for its new platform. Idei believed Kutaragi should lead this entire process.

Kutaragi, however, had a different idea of what Sony's strategy should be. Upon taking charge, Kutaragi forced the consumer electronics sector to adopt the management style used in the game business. Because he had invested up to 500 billion yen in Cell and wanted to recoup this cost, he forced all the other electronics business to use Cell in their products even though consumer electronics managers believed Cell was too powerful, too expensive, and emitted too much heat for most consumer electronics products. He did not understand the consumer electronics business and pushed to integrate game platforms and consumer electronics even when this was inappropriate. For instance, a product called Sugoroku, which was equipped with a hard disc and DVD and contained TV program recording functions, was perceived as competing against PSX, which is an upgraded version of PS2 with DVD functions. Kutaragi closed down the business division in charge of Sugoroku, which had sold better than PSX had, and further upgraded PSX by grafting Sugoroku's functions to PSX, a move that received criticism.[13]

Kutaragi cancelled Aiwa's USB player project and merged it with the personal audio business, which further delayed Sony's effort to develop MP3 players. The head of Sony's personal audio business, who was worried about his position being undermined if USB audio succeeded, influenced Kutaragi in this decision.[14] Kutaragi also closed the PTC (Platform Technology Center), which was researching and developing Internet services, copyright protection technologies, and next-generation operating systems—which was originally set up to push Idei's network strategy—and the NACS (Network Application and Contents Service) division, which researched the interface between hardware and content. Kutaragi disbanded NACS while it was still in its developmental phase and integrated it into the home electronics development business. This move nullified Idei's network strategy and instituted a vertical integration strategy on key components that Kutaragi was focused on. Kutaragi described this process as "creative destruction."[15]

Some have suggested that Kutaragi made these moves to undermine Idei and Ando so that he might become President himself. He was overtly critical of Idei at board meetings, where he contended that the network strategies Idei had pursued were all wrong.[16] Kutaragi further criticized both Idei and Ando for not investing in flat panel displays, openly commenting to the media that "We made a mistake in the transition time. We needed a big change."[17] Meanwhile, Ohga also openly expressed displeasure at Idei to journalists and Sony's employees, supporting Kutaragi's criticism and undermining Idei's position.

On March 7, 2005, Chairman Idei and President Ando resigned. All six internal board members followed, which meant that Kutaragi also had to resign. Kutaragi's power was limited to finishing the development of PlayStation 3, and he resigned soon after its release.[18] This decision was made by the Executive Nomination Committee, created by Idei, consisting of several outside directors, and had passed through the entire board. Because the outside directors had been appointed by Idei and

Outgoing and incoming management teams, Kunitake Ando, Nubuyuki Idei, Howard Stringer, Ryoji Chubachi, and Katsumi Ihara (from left to right). Photograph by Associated Press.

were heavily influenced by him, it could be said that in pulling down Kutaragi and nullifying Ohga, he also got rid of Ando and himself.

Sony's board nominated Howard Stringer and Ryoji Chubachi as the new chairman and president. Stringer had been in charge of restructuring Sony America and Sony Pictures since 1997. Chubachi, a former engineer, was managing the recording media business. Katsumi Ihara was nominated as vice president and CFO. All three men had been appointed by Idei. Chubachi defined his most urgent task as "the Renaissance of the Electronics Sector," and concentrated on producing electronic hardware, such as LCD TVs. He emphasized that Sony had to become a "modernized corporation"[19] that was "independent from past glory and the founders' shadow, and could be managed by ordinary people just like himself." In other words, he pursued a form of organization that was systematic, not charismatic.

### Applicability of a Western-Style Governance Structure

Sony's conversion to a Western board system was a benchmarking device, since Sony yearned to become a global corporation. As Sony grew larger, it also became harder for over thirty board members to make effective decisions. Ever since Sony adopted the Company Structure, individual business units were more settled in managing their own businesses. Idei may have thought the executives for each company should manage their respective operations, and the board could supervise the overall Group and decide its general direction. A board with outside directors with diverse backgrounds and experience has several possible benefits, such as preventing a CEO from making autocratic decisions. Its potential drawback is that outside directors may not be familiar with the industry itself, and therefore tend to evaluate performance based on short-term profitability. A board with diverse interests also may take a longer time to reach a consensus and tend be risk averse.

Many problems that Sony encountered, however, resulted from the attempt to transform Sony from a traditional Japanese firm into a Westernized global firm. Even though Sony implemented a Western board system, company structure, and evaluation measures like EVA, it is questionable whether Sony's executives and employees were ready to accept those systems and operate within them. At its heart, Sony remained a Japanese firm.

A Western corporate governance structure can be effective only when outside directors, managers, and employees, are ready to support such a system and social conditions are conducive. For conditions to be conducive, capital markets need to be well developed, shareholders should be dispersed, security analysts must closely scrutinize firms' performance, and societal expectations should be similar to those in Western countries. Under Sony's old board system, business division heads had the opportunity to meet to discuss and share business-related issues. They could resolve conflicts in advance and agree on areas for mutual cooperation. When Idei implemented the Western board system, however, these executives were excluded from the board. Divisional heads formed a 1:1 relationship with the CEO, and it grew more difficult to share interdivisional issues with other divisional heads. Sony's messy fight between two digital music players, separately developed by its VAIO and Personal Audio Companies, is only one such consequence.

Dividing Sony's top managerial powers in terms of CEO and COO titles added to the confusion.[20] Although these titles were standard in the United States, they were difficult for Japanese businesses to understand. In Japan, the president traditionally has full authority, in effect acting as the CEO. The chairman's position is often honorary, taken only after retirement. The proliferation of titles confused Sony's employees, as well as outsiders.

Even when Ohga was CEO and Idei president, Ohga decided whether to appoint executives, and Idei could not fully exercise his power. For instance, Idei constantly told his executives that the heyday for products such as MDs or the Walkman was over, and that they needed to develop network products to replace them. His managers did not understand why they had to develop such products when the current products were selling well. Unless they received a direct order from Ohga, division heads ignored Idei's orders, and Idei did not have the power to replace them because Ohga was the CEO. Even if Idei could have fired them, he would have had to take full responsibility for their division's performance if he could not find anyone who could do a better job.

Naturally, it was difficult to reform the organization. Middle managers were confused about whether to listen to Idei, or to wait for Ohga's instructions. After Ohga retired and Idei became the CEO, the relationship between Idei and President Ando also remained vague. Idei wanted to set a company-wide vision and have President Ando execute his strategies. Managers then often waited for Idei's direct orders rather than doing as President Ando ordered, which weakened President Ando's executive capacities. Idei's decision in 2003 to put Kutaragi in charge of the electronics, semiconductor, and game businesses further undermined Ando's position.

Sony's adoption of a Western governance structure entailed more costs than benefits. Sony's globalization reform was only superficial, and did not globalize Sony's system as it was supposed to. Idei's attempts to restructure and reform Sony overlooked the fact that Sony's management and employees were still fundamentally Japanese.

## Samsung's Powerful Owner-Centered Structure

### Emperor Management

The governance structures of Sony and Samsung are very distinct. Samsung's governance structure can be characterized by the powerful authority held by the chairman of Samsung Group. Chairman Lee's reign has sometimes been referred to as "emperor management" or "dictatorship." A Sony executive joked, "When Chairman Lee says something, it is like a God's voice, a sort of Divine voice. Everyone listens and nobody can say no." The benefit of this power structure is that it enabled the organization to make decisions quickly and aggressively, and take full responsibility for its strategies. This capacity has been a significant competitive advantage for Samsung Electronics.

Samsung Electronics has had several turning points when important strategic decisions were made under conditions of uncertainty. In 1987, for instance, there was a dispute in the semiconductor industry regarding whether to select the stack or trench method to develop 4M DRAMs.[21] Chairman Lee gathered advice from many engineers and decided on the stack method.[22] Later, his decision was proved right, and other firms in the industry used the stack method to produce 16M and 64M DRAMs. Yet Chairman Lee was not an engineer, and he received input from many others who were far more expert and experienced in the field. Companies tend to hesitate in making decisions when there is uncertainty, but timing is crucial in the semiconductor business. Samsung Electronics was able to make decisions swiftly and concentrate on improving efficiency because it had a centralized structure with the chairman as its head.

Chairman Lee's decisiveness again proved helpful when Samsung Electronics decided to deploy an 8-inch wafer processing line for its semiconductors in 1993. The industry standard at the time was a 6-inch production line. Eight-inch production lines were technically feasible, but it was uncertain whether one would succeed. Many opposed it, for a failure with the 8-inch line could cost over 1 trillion won.[23] Chairman Lee thought this investment would provide Samsung Electronics a good opportunity to catch up with market leaders, and he approved the investment. His decision became the turning point for Samsung Electronics, which rose above Japanese companies in the global market and became the market leader in the memory business.

President Yoon-woo Lee of Samsung Electronics' Semiconductor Division described the factors that led to his division's success in the memory semiconductor business: "I think the corporate governance system in Korea was in our favor, too. For this high-risk and high-return industry, the *chaebol* system worked well for us. Since Samsung was controlled by a charismatic leader, Chairman Lee, we could make this series of bold decisions. I think such bold decisions would not have been possible in other countries, where companies are controlled by professional managers. Memory is a business in which you cannot make a profit in the next upturn if you did not make a proper investment in the past. You need to make profits in the upturns to invest them for the next upturns. Thus, if you cannot invest properly according to a business cycle, you are not well prepared for the next one. If you miss this timing several times, then you quickly go out of business. Samsung could invest even in the downturns since Samsung was a *chaebol* company."[24]

In another incident, Chairman Lee ordered Samsung SDI, the original developer of LCD technology in Samsung Group, to transfer its LCD business to Samsung Electronics. He told his executives: "The LCD business will be transferred to Samsung Electronics. Samsung SDI should, instead, become number one in its CRT business by increasing its market share to 25% within three to four years. The LCD business requires a frontier spirit. Samsung SDI is diligent like a farmer, but its corporate culture doesn't fit creative work. The production process for LCDs is similar to that of semiconductors, so we can't leave the business to Samsung SDI just because they're displays. This business also requires huge investment, and Samsung SDI doesn't seem to have that capacity."[25] This episode shows the resoluteness of Chairman Lee, and it reveals the characteristics of Samsung's governing structure. Samsung Electronics and Samsung SDI were both listed companies, owned by separate shareholders, but the LCD business was transferred to Samsung Electronics with one word from Chairman Lee, even though Samsung SDI had already made significant progress. Samsung SDI gave up the LCD business to Samsung Electronics and has focused on PDPs instead.

## The Problems with Samsung's Governing Structure

### One-Man Decision-Making Structure

Samsung Electronics' governing structure is characterized by a powerful owner-centered system, and a staff organization that comprehensively supports his reign through financial, personnel, auditing, and planning processes (see Chapter 6). If, for instance, Samsung Electronics wishes to invest in a next-generation semiconductor line, Samsung Electronics' financial team reviews the proposal that is formulated and submitted by the business unit that wishes to make the investment, and hands it to the Group's Office of Secretaries, which evaluates it for Chairman Lee, who then approves or denies the proposal. Board of directors meetings or executive meetings offer a forum for consultation, but do not have ultimate decision-making power. Also, Samsung Electronics' outside directors are mostly members of Chairman Lee's inner circles, such as the head of the Group Office of Secretaries, Hak-su Lee; the CEO of Samsung Electronics, Jong-yong Yun; or former managers who are personal acquaintances of Chairman Lee. In 2006, six of Samsung Electronics' thirteen directors were executives of Samsung, and only one of the other seven directors is a foreigner. Other outside directors are either academics or lawyers who are closely involved in Samsung's business.

The problem Samsung Electronics' governance structure is the uncertainty of leadership; the late chairman, Byung-chull Lee, and the current chairman, Kun-hee Lee, have been "wise emperors," but there is no guarantee that such leadership will be sustained. Further, even "wise emperors" make mistakes, such as Chairman Kun-hee Lee's decision to enter the automobile industry in 1993. Chairman Kun-hee Lee recalls: "I agonized over many days and nights whether to enter the automobile industry. Many were opposed, saying there was no reason to start such a complex business when others including the semiconductor sector were doing so well. Another factor I had to think about was the immense risk involved with this huge investment. In fact, there is no reason to take such pains, if I think just of Samsung and myself. But considering our economy, in which exports are essential, and the level of development in our automobile industry, I thought someone had to enter and upgrade the overall industry…. I studied the automobile industry more than anyone else, and met numerous people. I read almost all the automobile magazines one can think of, and met every single engineer and upper-level manager from major car makers. I hadn't begun Samsung's automobile business impromptu, but had been thoroughly preparing and researching about this…."[26]

Although Chairman Lee made what he believed was a careful, reasoned decision, he overlooked several important concerns that made it unlikely Samsung Group could succeed in this market. By 1993, the global automobile industry was consolidating and rationalizing. Some observers believed that only about 10 companies would be able to survive, due to the economies of scale required to develop and produce new cars. Major European car makers such as Volvo, Saab, and Rover had been acquired by global enterprises such as Ford or GM. The fledgling Samsung had no chance of surviving.

The automobile business inflicted a huge loss on the Group, and Samsung Motors was sold to Renault in 1999. It is likely that few were courageous enough to oppose Chairman Lee's decision when it was first announced, especially since his resoluteness had been crucial to the semiconductor business' success. In fact, some executives who expressed concerns about this business venture were fired. Under an "emperor management" system, the leader can make both inspired and disastrous decisions.

Jae-yong Lee, the son of Chairman Lee, has not had a promising record thus far. He invested in Internet startups during the dot.com bubble and suffered huge losses. Eventually, several Samsung affiliates took over those startups and bailed him out. Further, Samsung Electronics' challenges are different now from what they were in the past. Because the firm was a latecomer to the electronics industry and technological trajectories were clear, it was not difficult for it to figure out what to do: catching up with market leaders through hard work and ingenuity was enough. Right now, however, Samsung Electronics is a leader, not a follower. Because it has so many different strategic options for further growth, an autocratic system may no longer be optimal. The most urgent task for Samsung Electronics at this point is to find out how the company can assist the leader's decision making, how others can present diverse opinions, and what should be done to reduce the risk of wrong decisions.

### Sustainability of Family Control

Chairman Kun-hee Lee is a second-generation family owner. He became chairman after Chairman Byung-chull Lee passed away in 1987. When it is stated that Chairman Lee is an owner, it does not mean that he owns a majority of shares in Samsung Group. He and his family own less than 4% of all Samsung Group's shares. Yet they rule over 60 subsidiaries, as if they owned 100%, because of the cross-shareholding among Samsung affiliates, which amounts to 22%. Figure 7.1 shows the ownership pattern of Samsung Group. Figure 7.2 is a simplified

Kun-hee Lee, Chairman of Samsung Group (center); his wife, Na-hee Hong (left); and his son, Jae-yong Lee (right). Photograph by Chosun Ilbo.

*Figure 7.1*   Ownership structure of top 25 Samsung affiliates

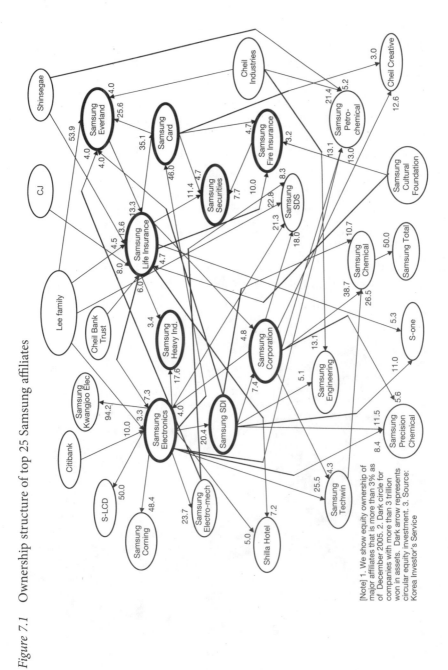

[Note] 1. We show equity ownership of major affiliates that is more than 3% as of December 2005. 2. Dark circle for companies with more than 3 trillion won in assets. Dark arrow represents circular equity investment. 3. Source: Korea Investor's Service

*Figure 7.2* Ownership Structure around Samsung Electronics

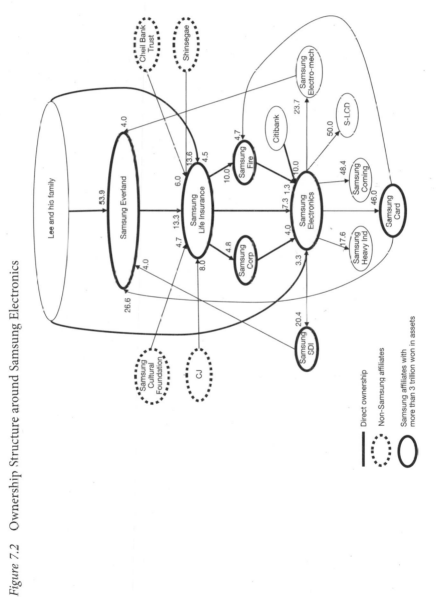

version of 7.1, focusing around Samsung Electronics; Chairman Lee's family is a major shareholder of Samsung Everland, a privately owned firm; Samsung Everland owns Samsung Life, which is also an unlisted firm, and Samsung Life owns a large share in Samsung Electronics. Under this governing structure, Jae-yong Lee is preparing to succeed his father as chairman. Samsung is under scrutiny, however, for how it has structured the inheritance process around the Lee family.

As of 1999, Chairman Lee's wealth was estimated to be two trillion won, and his son's wealth was estimated to be several hundred billion won. Jae-young Lee was still a student and had never run a business. When he inherited assets worth several hundred billion won, he paid an inheritance tax of only 1.6 billion won. His increase in wealth is attributable to the large capital gains of IPO stocks. Figure 7.3 shows that Jae-young Lee inherited 6 billion won from Kun-hee Lee in December 1995. This gift is the only instance of Kun-hee Lee officially giving cash to his son. After paying the inheritance tax, Jae-young Lee used the remaining 4.4 billion won to purchase stocks of unlisted affiliates in Samsung Group. He bought 124,800 shares of S-one, a home security company, with 2.3 billion won and 470,000 shares of Samsung Engineering with 1.9 billion won. When these firms were listed on the stock market several months later, the value of his stock in them was 35.7 billion won and 23 billion won, respectively. He sold these shares for 52.7 billion won, or 12 times his original investment.

Using these proceeds, he bought convertible bonds of Cheil Communication, then unlisted, worth 1.8 billion won. These bonds were subsequently converted into stock that gave him 29.7% ownership of the company. When Cheil Communication was listed on the stock market in March 1998, his investment of 1.8 billion won soared to 15.3 billion won. He also purchased convertible bonds in Samsung Everland for far less than their market price. These bonds were then converted to a 31.9% equity stake in this firm, which then used the proceeds of this convertible bond issue to purchase 20% ownership in Samsung Life, which is one of the core holding companies in the Samsung Group. He also bought 23 billion won of convertible bonds issued by Samsung SDS at the issue price of 7,150 won, which was far below the then-market price of 54,000 won. As Samsung SDS is soon to be listed, the value of this investment is anticipated to increase by 20 times the acquisition price. Furthermore, he invested 45 billion

*Figure 7.3* Transfer of Wealth through Insider Information

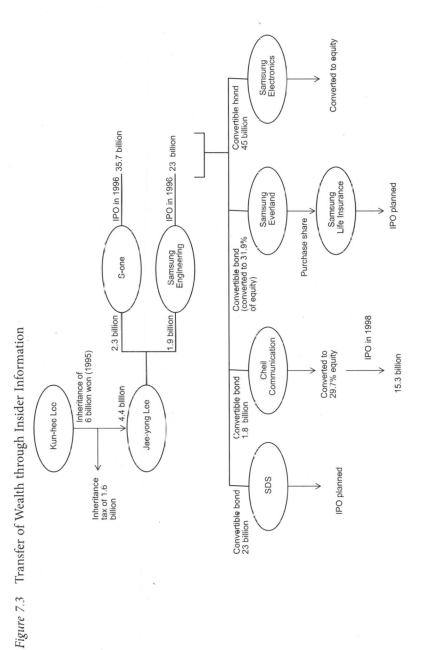

won to buy convertible bonds of Samsung Electronics. The convertible bonds were issued at a below-market price and provided high interest rates. He then converted these bonds to stock, thus securing 0.78% of Samsung Electronics.

Such activities capitalize on loopholes in the Korean tax system that let family members inherit wealth and managerial control without a heavy tax burden. They also take away the assets of minority shareholders of listed firms. Furthermore, buying shares of unlisted companies at low prices and reaping large capital gains after these firms are listed is a clear abuse of insider information and represents another facet of the agency problems in *chaebols'* governance structure. This case is under scrutiny, and is waiting to be resolved in court. In 2006, a new law was enacted that constrains the voting power of financial service firms. According to this new law, Samsung Everland—a private firm whose original business was in amusement parks and golf courses—would be reclassified as a financial service firm, which will make a big impact on Samsung Group's ownership structure.

Samsung Electronics also supports other affiliates of the Samsung Group, as a core group company, in various ways, against the interests of minority shareholders. It once explored the possibility of registering on the NYSE, which would be difficult for it to do given its complex ownership structure and unclear governance structure. For instance, Samsung Electronics has supported Samsung Card, a consumer financing affiliate, by owning shares and by providing additional equity capital. In 2003, it invested $700 million and in 2005 it invested another $557 million in this unrelated group affiliate. For Western firms, it would be difficult to justify this kind of investment in a firm that was unprofitable and completely unrelated to its own business. The bailout of Jae-yong Lee's failed Internet startups by Samsung affiliates is another instance of the Group's obscure governance system.

Shareholders of Samsung Electronics were not happy about these investments, and Samsung's responses to their concerns thus far have added fuel to the fire. At a shareholders' meeting, Samsung Electronics' CEO Yun said to angry minority shareholders, "Just how many shares do you have? Stop saying 'our' company!" Rather than serving shareholders, his loyalties seem to be to Chairman Lee. An investor from an asset management company in Singapore pointed out, "The company is majority held by foreign shareholders now but it is still run as a family concern."[27]

## The Inner Circle within Samsung

As discussed earlier, the Office of Secretaries is a very powerful organization within Samsung Group. Beyond the formal influence it exerts, it holds a considerable amount of informal pull. Approximately 100 people are part of the Office. They were selected out of talent pools, and usually spend a couple of years working for the Office and are then moved to individual affiliates, in which they take key positions. These individuals are smart and capable, but the most important quality for selection is loyalty to the Group chairman. There is a trust-based relation among people who went through the Office of Secretaries. They share information among themselves and often support each other in daily interactions. Hak-soo Lee, who is the head of the Office of Secretaries, is feared by executives, because he carries out Chairman Lee's orders. Some even criticize him for exercising power beyond the authority that Chairman Lee has given him.

By definition, this informal organization excludes ordinary employees. The decisions of its members, often positioned in finance, planning, and HR functions, carry more weight. These members also think similarly, raising the possibility of groupthink. In their ranks are the presidents of Samsung affiliates: Dong-man Bae of Cheil Communications; Woo-hee Lee of S-one; In Kim of Samsung SDS; Jing-wan Kim of Samsung Heavy Industries; Hyung-do Lee of Samsung Electro-mechanics; Young-ro Song of Samsung Corning; Bok-hyun Ahn of Samsung BP; Soon-taek Kim of Samsung SDI; Sung-ryeol Yoo of Samsung Card; and many others. It is no secret that a stint with the Office of Secretaries is a must to be promoted to senior management.

The other group of power elites is a group of engineers, often holding doctorate degrees from U.S. universities, who built their careers in R&D and production, and maintained Samsung Electronics' technical expertise. Beyond these two elite groups, sales and marketing people have not been well-regarded. For instance, Hak-soo Lee and Ji-sung Choi are both from the Office of Secretaries; all other executives above the level of Corporate Vice President are either engineers or managers who went through the Office of Secretaries. The situation is almost the same in other Samsung affiliates. In 2005, the Group reported the promotion of executives; among the 39 promoted above the level of senior executive directors, 31 were from either R&D or the administrative side, which consisted mainly of planning, HR, and finance.[28]

### Leadership of Professional Managers

A thorny problem of Samsung Electronics' corporate governance structure is the lack of leadership by professional managers, whose authority has been undermined by the Office of Secretaries. Because Chairman Lee makes all the important decisions in Samsung Group, the CEOs of Samsung affiliates have not learned to develop an overall view of their subsidiaries. Their ability to manage these companies is limited to making operating decisions under the parameters set by the Office of Secretaries. It is not clear whether professional managers can exercise sufficiently strong leadership if Samsung Group's succession plan does not go smoothly and Mr. Jae-yong Lee does not become a wise emperor. And so Samsung Electronics should foster talented

Jong-yong Yun, CEO (left), and Do-seok Choi CFO (right), of Samsung Electronics. Photograph by Chosun Ilbo.

professional managers-cum-leaders who can effectively replace the Chairman's control.

Yet Chairman Lee's powers to promote, demote, hire, and fire at will further complicate the development of professional managers. Even Yun, the CEO of Samsung Electronics, does not know when he will be replaced, or by whom. The situation in Samsung Electronics, and the Samsung Group more generally, is like a court drama in which the emperor makes his subordinates compete with each other and divides and governs them with their loyalty as collateral. As a consequence, all executives compete against one another rather than cooperate, while Chairman Lee remains above them and coordinates them through his solemn orders. For example, presidents of Samsung Electronics' business divisions compete fiercely with each to show higher performances. According to Samsung insiders, price negotiation across business divisions, for instance between Digital Media Division producing MP3 players and the Semiconductor Division producing flash memory, is so tough and even hostile that it is hard to believe that they belong to the same company. Oftentimes, the only way to resolve conflicts between them is to bring up the issue to the Group Secretary Office and eventually to Chairman Lee. It looks as if the synergy among Samsung's divisions depends entirely upon Chairman Lee and his Secretary Office. Sony's experience in the transition from the founder generation to professional managers has demonstrated the perils of confusion in this process. Samsung Electronics should prepare itself in advance to avoid similar confusion when this transition is necessary.

# 8

# The Future of Sony and Samsung Electronics

Sony must become a "modernized company." A modernized company means a company that stands independent from the past glories, and the founders; a company that can be managed by ordinary people like myself. In other words, it means a company operated on a system.

—*President Chubachi, Sony*[1]

Now, other companies will no longer teach or lend us their technologies. That means Samsung must now do everything on its own, from technology development to establishing management systems. That process will be a lonely race.

—*Chairman Kun-hee Lee, Samsung Group*[2]

The differences in performance between Sony and Samsung Electronics are not the results of their strategies. Rather, organizational processes and executives' leadership seem to have determined their performances. In other words, Sony's digital dream kids' strategies could have worked if they had been executed properly. The fit between Samsung's strategy in responding to commoditization with speed and its militaristic organization may have contributed to its stellar performance.

Sony and Samsung Electronics have a good deal to learn from each other. From Sony, Samsung Electronics might learn how to transition from having founders rule the firm to letting professional managers take charge and how to change from a small domestic company into a large, far-flung global enterprise. Samsung Electronics could also learn from mistakes that Sony has made, which might help it resolve some of the long-term problems that it faces. On the other hand, Sony can learn from Samsung about how it can improve the execution and implementation of its strategy.

## Superficial Crisis and Internal Crisis

### The Internal Crisis of Samsung Electronics

Although Samsung Electronics is a competitive global enterprise, it is facing a serious internal crisis. One of its problems is excessive centralization. The major decision-making power is held by Chairman Lee and his Office of Secretaries, a group-level staff organization. There are no measures to check their decisions even when they take the wrong direction. In Western companies, strong corporate governance structures guard against such absolute power. These firms have boards of directors that appoint CEOs, determine their remuneration, and approve major investments. This system has been developed to prevent firms from being run into the ground by a few managers. In some Western countries, labor unions also influence a company's major decisions. Furthermore, the media and investment analysts also serve as a check against untrammeled executive power. In Korea, however, Samsung Group is extremely influential, and the media praises everything it does.

Currently, Samsung Electronics' board has only relatives of Samsung's founder and key senior executives on its board of directors. Also, although Jong-yong Yun's nominal title is CEO of Samsung Electronics, he is really a COO; he receives instructions from and is supervised by the Office of Secretaries, and Chairman Lee decides what Samsung Electronics' major strategic investments will be. The danger of Lee's power is exemplified by Samsung Group's ill-advised foray into the automobile industry during the mid-1990s. After losing a lot of money, Samsung Group sold the business to Renault. There was no one to oppose Lee's decision to enter this business. Although Lee's resolute decision making is considered important to Samsung Electronics' success, it may be a positive influence only when Samsung Electronics competes in businesses with clear technological trajectories, for which rapid development and production efficiency are essential. When businesses require creativity and have no clear evolutionary path, this one-man decision making may prove disastrous.

Samsung Electronics is also experiencing organizational fatigue, which has been induced by "fear-based management." Its employees and board members can be dismissed for any reason by the chairman, the Office of Secretaries, or other superior managers. The Office of Secretaries (renamed the Group Strategic Planning Office in 2007) monitors key executives' performance. Working under such stress, Samsung's employees are suffering accumulated fatigue. Indeed, despite its status as the best company in Korea, over 10% of Samsung Electronics' employees quit their jobs in their first year and over 30% do so by their third year because they are unable to bear the heavy workload. Samsung Electronics' parts suppliers, including other Samsung Group affiliates, are also under great pressure to comply with Samsung Electronics' demands to lower costs and meet delivery deadlines.

A lack of creativity is another of Samsung Electronics' weaknesses. So long as it had a clear target to pursue, such as Sony in consumer electronics, Intel in semiconductors, and Nokia in the mobile phone business, it could surmount its considerable disadvantages by benchmarking against these firms and having its employees work around the clock. The firm's corporate culture, management goals, values, and management resources have been optimized to capitalize on the benefits available to a late entrant.

As it has become a market leader, however, there is no one for it to imitate. Instead, it must lead by developing new technology and formulating innovative corporate strategies. Yet it has few creative employees who can generate genuinely new ideas. Furthermore, both engineers and managers fear failures, which make them focus on projects that may have immediate payback and low risk. Even worse, Samsung Electronics has thus far failed to accumulate technical expertise in developing new products because its R&D divisions have been focusing primarily on improving production efficiency.

Chairman Lee is aware of the "creativity gap," especially in regard to personnel, and has taken various initiatives to close it. Since 2002, he has had every subsidiary report monthly its record of securing key talent, and these records are factored in to evaluations of the respective subsidiary presidents' performance. Lee also made "creativity" the core creed for management in 2006. Currently, about 4,000 of Samsung Group's employees are considered "key members"; Samsung Electronics has about 2,800 of them. These employees are ranked as S(super), A(ace), and H(high potential), and receive special attention.

Beyond closing the creativity gap, Samsung Electronics must deepen the pool of talent that it needs to become a global enterprise. So far, it has been able to satisfy this need by hiring Koreans or Korean-Americans. Yet such people are in short supply, and are increasingly harder to find. Unless Samsung Electronics becomes more serious about hiring and promoting non-Koreans and/or purchasing firms that have promising technologies and good managers, its lack of talent in the global arena could fetter its growth.

Furthermore, Samsung Electronics shows signs of hubris. In the past, Samsung Electronics, as a late entrant, tried to maintain a willingness to learn from others. As it enjoys good performance and is acknowledged as an industry leader, however, it has become less inclined to correct its internal problems. "Samsung is having a Sony moment"—a comment by a cynic suggests that Samsung Electronics is showing signs of complacency just as Sony did 10 years ago.[3] Indeed, Samsung's performance did begin to deteriorate in 2007 due to intensified competition in memory chips and LCDs.

### Sony's Ordeals and Potentials

Chairman Stringer officially admitted that Sony's problems have resulted from strategic and organizational failures. Stringer believed that Sony's organization has become too divided and that its business units have become silos, which has made resource allocation less efficient, added to Sony's bureaucracy, and slowed decision making. He argued that Sony needed both to develop a strategic focus and to create competitive advantage by developing new products.[4] Stringer introduced an internal slogan, "Sony United," to promote teamwork, cooperation, and the marriage of key resources.

To these ends, he dissolved the Network Company structure that Idei had implemented, converted it back to the traditional business division structure, and centralized the decision-making process in order to break down internal barriers and to encourage communication across businesses. Control over product planning, purchasing, and technology development was transferred back to President Chubachi; instead of being parceled out over far-flung divisions, Sony's resources were concentrated on developing new hit products. According to Stringer and Chubachi, "this significant structural change was designed to eliminate the business 'silos' and to foster a more coordinated, efficient and rapid decision-making process."[5] They also decided to close 11 out of 65 factories to save 200 billion yen, and ordered the layoffs of 10,000 employees by March 2008. They are still considering whether to close or rationalize factories in the United States, the UK, China, and Japan.

Nonetheless, Sony still has formidable technology, know-how, and human talent. Its failure to develop new products since the mid-1990s has stemmed mainly from its organization and leadership, rather than from its lack of technological capacity. The patents and technologies Sony retains should lead to good short-term performance if Sony can overcome its recent setbacks. Moreover, Sony has a strong brand. Although one study found that Sony's brand value was declining, that study measured brand value in conjunction with the brand's financial performance (see Chapter 4). Other studies suggest that Sony remains one of the highest-ranked brands.

Also, although Sony has not been able to create synergies between its hardware and entertainment businesses, it may regain that opportunity soon if digital convergence further unites content, hardware, and communication businesses. If this occurs, Sony's portfolio is ideal, since it encompasses businesses in audio and video home electronics, computers, communications, games, film, and music, as well as a strong brand image. If Sony can exploit this potential, it will possess an extraordinary competitive edge. If it cannot, Sony has to consider seriously an option to break up the company by spinning off the entertainment and game businesses, not to mention its insurance and financial services units. A stand-alone electronics unit may enable its workers to focus on the dynamics of digital technology.

## Lessons Learned by Sony and Samsung Electronics

### The Focusing Strategy of a Latecomer

What made Samsung Electronics a global brand in the last decade was its strategic "selection and concentration." It learned the lessons of aggressive investment and fast execution in the DRAM business and applied them to flash memory and LCDs, which, like DRAM, had industry standards, involved mature technologies, and were quickly commoditized. It also used technology that it could buy from other firms. This strategy, a far cry from Sony's goal of creating unique products, compensated for Samsung's shortage of technological know-how, and allowed Samsung to reap the maximum benefit from its workforce.

Samsung Electronics was also quick to exploit the opportunities of digital technology. Because there is no difference in the quality of digital products so long as each uses the same chip set, Samsung Electronics could catch up with market leaders even though it was a late entrant and was technologically inferior in the analog world. It then allocated its marketing resources in order to improve its brand image and concentrated most of these resources in mobile phones, which was the product for which it could get the highest return on its investment. In choosing distribution channels in foreign markets, Samsung Electronics focused on selling to a small number of specialty electronics stores, adopted a high-price, high-margin strategy, and gave dealers incentives to sell its products. It also realigned its sales organizations in big cities and selected "emerging markets" around the world in which to market. What differentiated Samsung Electronics' marketing activities from those of Sony is that Samsung actively invested in marketing, and Sony did not. Sony's brand value came mainly from the company's capabilities in new product development. In contrast, Samsung Electronics erected its brand out of nothing, despite the poor quality of its products, by strategically investing in marketing and distribution.

Other late entrants can learn from Samsung Electronics' experience. Typically, late entrants try to catch up with market leaders by benchmarking them and imitating their strategies. This strategy is doomed to failure, however, because late entrants, which have fewer resources and less technological capability, can never catch up with leaders simply by imitating them. Samsung Electronics' story demonstrates that a company can create competitive advantage by using paradigm shifts such as the advent of digitalization to concentrate its resources in technologies, products, markets, and channels that play to its unique strengths.

## Core Competences and the Competence Trap

Both Sony and Samsung Electronics demonstrate that a firm's core competence can easily become its core liability.[6] Samsung Electronics makes decisions swiftly and has an execution-oriented corporate culture. These factors are common to many Korean companies, as well as to military organizations. Once the head of the organization makes a decision, the organization focuses all its effort on achieving these goals without complaints or contemplation. Samsung Electronics' other core competence is its production efficiency. It is the world's most cost-efficient producer of memory and LCDs. This advantage originates from its investments in production facilities and process technology, which reduces costs and enhances yield.

Yet these strengths are also Samsung Electronics' weaknesses. The firm's corporate culture of obedience and execution and its strong financial orientation may be rapid and efficient, but they also hinder new product development and creativity. Compared to Sony, Samsung Electronics is weak in nonmemory businesses and end products, for which creativity is required. Its end products compete on cost; they are not different from competitors' offerings. This weakness happens because the firm takes practices that are appropriate for the memory business and applies them to nonmemory ones and end products.

Unlike Samsung, Sony excels in developing original new products under its founding creed of "Freedom and Open-mindedness." Its liberal, vibrant corporate culture made Sony an engineers' heaven. Sony's engineers researched what they were interested in, and the technologies they developed gave birth to innovative new products like the Walkman, CDs, DVDs, 8mm camcorders, digital cameras, PlayStation, and Aibo. This culture requires extensive trial and error, however, until the final result is achieved. Innovation can be costly, time-consuming, and inefficient. Also, because Sony engineers were free to do what they wanted, they often concentrated on technology that was unrealistic or hard-to-commercialize. In short, Sony's organization was fit for developing new technologies and products, but was unsuitable for executing the CEO's strategies. Sony has fallen not because Idei's network strategy was ill-advised; it has fallen because the organization is incapable of executing strategies.

The case of Sony and Samsung Electronics also illustrates how difficult it is for a firm to forgo its past success and transform its culture to meet changing environments. Idei commented, "The difficulty Sony faced was that we could not forget the success of the past. Sony's success was based on the tape format, CD format, and transistor TV. People complain, 'In old days, we were clearly a leader but what are we now?' But, the world is changing. The probable difficulty of Samsung in the future will be how they can forget the success of the past, such as the success of DRAM, LCD, and mobile telecom?"

## Fit of Corporate Culture, Organization, and Leadership

Sony got into trouble under Idei because his leadership did not complement Sony's corporate culture and organization. Sony's corporate culture of "freedom and open-mindedness" and independent business units worked well under Morita not because Sony was systematically managed but because of Morita's charisma. Morita could interfere with matters and placate complaints and uncertainty when there were conflicts among company units or business prospects were hazy.

Because Idei was Sony's first salary-man president, however, it was difficult both to expect him to have charisma and to expect his subordinates would unconditionally obey him. Idei understood his limits as a professional manager and tried to realign the organization to reflect those limits. His policies, such as the company system, a board with outside directors, and the separation of executives from board members came from his intention to operate Sony, a giant conglomerate by that time, without relying on charisma. Sony's corporate culture and management style could not be changed easily, however, so Idei's efforts were unsuccessful.

In sum, Sony's stagnation during the last decade may be the result of the mismatch of its strategy, leadership style, corporate culture, and organizational structure. By contrast, Samsung Electronics' stellar performance may derive from the close connection between its strategy of accepting commoditization while creating competitive advantages in speed, and its execution-oriented organization under a charismatic leader. Samsung's corporate culture, emphasizing loyalty and discipline, also made it easier to effect its strategies.

### Conversion from a Family-Owned Company to a Professional Management System

Sony's mismatch is also attributable to the difficult transition from the founders' generation to a generation of professional managers. Idei once lamented that, despite the fact that Sony had grown up to a half a hundred billion dollar company, it was still driven by the founders' vision: "I knew that running Sony was impossible because it was a company driven by the founders' vision: the founders' personal vision was the basis and the standard for every decision." This comment suggests the biggest challenge Idei faced: to satisfy employees' expectations, which had been fostered by the founders. He had to do so despite being Sony's first president who had begun as a salary-man, in addition to meeting the technological challenges that digital innovation and network technology posed. Ibuka, Sony's founder, was a great engineer, and Morita was an extraordinary manager. Ohga, although not a founder, was also considered part of the founders' generation, because he had joined Sony so close to its founding. In addition, Ohga was accomplished. He was a vocalist, and a friend of world-famous musicians, and had even once conducted the Berlin Philharmonic. He also had a pilot's license, and was a legendary manager who achieved great success with the PlayStation, despite internal opposition.

In contrast, Idei did not have as distinguished a past, and he was the lowest-ranked, youngest executive member when he was appointed. While he presented his strategic vision, he did not have enough charisma to sell it to his employees, and so he failed to meet their expectations. Ohga nominated Idei based on his personal judgment; he did not do so after thorough preparation and verification. Idei did not have sufficient time to prepare for his new position. Consequently, his leadership was challenged, and he could not realize his vision.

This confusion during the succession process provides a good lesson to other companies, including Samsung Electronics. Sony's misfortune might have started with Morita's sudden illness. He could not talk and lay in bed for six years, during which there was a vacuum of top management leadership. A top Sony executive said, "Illness is something you cannot control. Because of it, Sony had a dramatic succession. Morita was like a God. No one could possibly replace him."

Many firms throughout the world are managed by founders with strong charisma. It is critical for these firms to learn to replace the irreplaceables. Chubachi's comments that Sony must become a modernized company, operated on a system and managed by an ordinary person like himself, succinctly summarize the challenges of all firms that are undergoing the transition to a new generation of leaders. Perhaps, another challenge for Chubachi is to learn how a company run by an ordinary man can continue to be extraordinary in the future. For example, in 2006 Toshitada Doi, a famed engineer, resigned after his pet project, Aibo, a robot dog, was terminated. More than 100 Sony employees then threw a mock funeral for the Aibo. At the funeral ceremony, Doi recalled, "Aibo was a symbol of a risk-taking spirit [of Sony] that was now dead."[7] Sony has been a very extraordinary company by any measure. It can be managed by an ordinary man, to use Chubachi's phrase. It will not be possible to keep generating innovative products without the risk-taking Sony spirit. The greatest challenge for Stringer and Chubachi will be to maintain the Sony spirit.

Chairman Lee is a second-generation member of Samsung Group's founding family. It is not clear whether his family can maintain its "emperor management" control over the Samsung Group in the future. Lee and his family members own less than 4% of Samsung Group, and own even less of Samsung Group's listed companies. Moreover, with over 50% of Samsung Electronics' stocks owned by foreign investors, and as Samsung's subsidiaries become larger, it will grow more difficult to run Samsung Electronics as if it were a family-owned company. It will be interesting to see whether Samsung Electronics can maintain its core competence of orderly, responsive management when professional managers begin running Samsung Group. To prevent the confusion and errors that can occur, as they did in Sony, during this transition, Samsung must foster professional managers and establish a systematic governance structure in advance.

## Challenges in Becoming a Global Enterprise

Sony has taken many steps toward globalization. It has developed and sold its products worldwide, acquired U.S. entertainment firms, implemented a Western-style board of directors, and even hired a foreigner as its CEO. Although these facts show how globalized Sony appears from the outside, it is questionable whether Sony's internal globalization, such as the mindset of the employees, is at the same level.

The likely causes for Sony's current problems are legion. Sony was driven by the founder's vision rather than by a systematic plan, and the organization was run based on personal relationships. It could be said that Sony's loss of control over Sony America happened because Sony promoted globalization and localization too rapidly, without considering its competence to manage the inevitable tension of its global localization strategy. Moreover, Sony's globalization may have reflected its overconfidence about its capacity for globalized management. Its adoption of COO and CEO titles from Western companies may have been unwise because most of Sony's employees perceived the president to be the CEO. This mismatch created confusion over who had ultimate power. Also, the company system turned traditionally independent departments into silos, and short-term performance indexes such as EVA hindered long-term investments such as R&D. Sony's experience shows how dangerous "visible" or "superficial globalization" can be.

Sony's problems might have stemmed from globalization that was too rapid, but Samsung Electronics' biggest problem may be its procrastination about globalizing. However grand and global its production and distribution goals are, its employees' ability to manage global operations is limited. It will also need to discard its Korean bias and hire more creative talent from other countries, because the Korean educational system does not foster creative engineers and managers. Achieving these goals will not be easy, especially because Samsung Electronics is currently enjoying its heyday. Because of its outstanding performance and the worldwide adulation it is receiving, hubris is growing within the organization and undermining the company's ability to look critically at itself and correct its mistakes. This arrogance, the pride that anything Samsung does is bound to be the best, the sense that Samsung is now a first-class global corporation that has nothing to learn from others, reminds some observers of Sony 10 years ago. Samsung Electronics must remember that in order to truly win at global competition, it must face and overcome even greater challenges in the years ahead.

# Endnotes

## Chapter 1

1    Foroohar, R., and B. Lee. Masters of the Digital Age. *Newsweek*, October 11, 2004, p. 33.

2    Porter, M. What Is Strategy? *Harvard Business Review*, (1996), 74(6), 61–78.

3    Solomon J. Seoul Survivors: Back From Brink, Korea Inc. Wants A Little Respect—Samsung Is Reborn as Maker of Upscale Electronics; It Seeks Image to Match—Case of the Missing Billboard, *Wall Street Journal*, June 13, 2002, p. A.1.

4    Edwards, C., I. Moon, and P. Engardio. The Samsung Way. *BusinessWeek*, June 16, 2003, p. 48.

5    Mossberg, W. S. Shaking Up Sony. *Wall Street Journal*, June 6, 2006, p. B.1.

6    Edwards, C., T. Lowry, I. Moon, and K. Hall. The Lessons For Sony At Samsung. *BusinessWeek*, October 10, 2005, p. 35.

7    Fisher, A., and J. Kahn. The World's Most Admired Companies. *Fortune*, October 27, 1997, p. 220.

8    The Best & Worst Managers of The Year. *BusinessWeek*, January 12, 2004, p. 73.

9    Ibid.

10   Moon, I. Samsung a Korean Giant Confronts the Crisis. *BusinessWeek*, March 23, 1998, p. 18.

11    Kraar, L. The Man Who Shook Up Samsung. *Fortune*, January 24, 2000, p. 28.

12    Bennett, P., C. Chandler, T. Demos, J. Elliott, E. Ellis, R. Horn, C. Kano, and A. Taylor. Asia's 25 Most Powerful. *Fortune*, October 17, 2005, p. 56.

13    Peters, T., and R. Waterman. *In Search of Excellence: Lessons from America's Best-Run Companies*. New York: Warner Books, 1982; Collins, J. *Good to Great: Why Some Companies Make the Leap and Others Don't*. New York: Random House Business Books, 2001; Collins, J., and J. Porras. *Built to Last: Successful Habits of Visionary Companies*. New York: HarperBusiness, 1994.

14    Rosenzweig, P. *The Halo Effect*. New York: Free Press, 2007.

15    Edwards, C., I. Moon, and P. Engardio. The Samsung Way. *BusinessWeek*, June 16, 2003. p. 52.

16    Sony Annual Report, 2006, p. 28.

17    Samsung Electronics is proud of being No. 1 in the global market in 2006, including its LCD TVs, PDP TVs, and color TVs. It holds 14.2% of the global market share, which surpasses Sony's 11.3% and LG Electronics' 8.6% (*Joong Ang Ilbo*, February 14, 2007).

18    Belton, B. Stringer on "the Sony Spirit." *BusinessWeek Online*, March 10, 2005.

19    Edwards, C., T. Lowry, I. Moon, and K. Hall. The Lessons For Sony At Samsung. *BusinessWeek*, October 10, 2005, p. 35.

20    Brull, S. V., N. Gross, and R. Hof. Sony's New World. *BusinessWeek*, May 27, 1996, p. 36.

21    Bremner, B., C. Edwards, R. Grover, T. Lowry, E. Thornton. Sony's Sudden Samurai. *BusinessWeek*, March 21, 2005.

22    Cho, H., H. Jeon, and S. Lim. *The Digital Conqueror Samsung Electronics* (in Korean). Seoul: *Maeil Economic News Press*, 2005, p. 192.

23    Edwards, C., T. Lowry, I. Moon, and K. Hall. The Lessons For Sony At Samsung. *BusinessWeek*, October 10, 2005. p. 35.

24    Porter, M. *Competitive Strategy*. New York: Free Press, 1980.

25    Allison, G. *Essence of Decision: Explaining the Cuban Missile Crisis*. Boston: Little, Brown and Company, 1971.

26.   Mintzberg argues that strategies deduced through rational analysis (deliberate strategy) do not generate results as planned and that the actual strategies that firms use are often impromptu ideas (emergent strategy) based on the given situation. According to Mintzberg, companies cannot formulate perfect strategies, and a CEO cannot completely control his entire organization because lower-level managers are often cut off from senior managers. Instead, strategy formulation is a kind of "crafting," rather than an elaborate planning. See Mintzberg, H. and, J. Waters.

Of Strategies: Deliberate and Emergent. *Strategic Management Journal*, (1985) 6, 257-272 and Mintzberg, H. Crafting Strategy, *Harvard Business Review* (1987), 65(4), 66-75.

## Chapter 2

1    Ohga, N. *Sony Bombs Hollywood* (Korean edition, Original Title: *Sony No Senritsu*). Seoul: Ruby Box, 2004, p. 281.

2    Chang, S., and P. Podolny, Samsung Electronics' Semiconductor Division, Stanford Business School Case IB24 (A) & (B), 2002.

3    Sony Promotion Division. *Sony Autobiography* (Korean edition, Original Title: *Sony Jijoden*). Seoul: SangSangBooks, 1998, p. 38.

4    Sony Promotion Division, 1998, op. cit. p. 155.

5    Ibid., 156.

6    Morita, A., E. M. Reingold, and M. Shimomura, *Made in Japan: Akio Morita and Sony*. London: Collins, 1987, p. 170.

7    Esaki, a Sony engineer, found a new phenomenon for transistors, and was awarded the Nobel Prize for it, but this is an exceptional case.

8    Rocks, D. Sony's Picture Looks Brighter. *BusinessWeek*, November 8, 2004, p. 64.

9    Belton, B. Stringer on "the Sony Spirit." *BusinessWeek Online*, March 10, 2005.

10   The patents Sony retained for CDs generated patent royalties over 20 billion yen each year.

11   Tateishi, Y. *Sony Inside Story* (in Japanese). Tokyo: Kudansha, 2006, ch.3.

12   Kang, J. *The Myth of Samsung Electronics and Its Secrets* (in Korean). Seoul: Kyryoone Publishing, 1996, p. 102.

13   Lee, K. *Kun-hee Lee Essay: Let's Think Before We Look at the World* (in Korean). Seoul: Donga Ilbo, 1997, p. 16.

14   For example, Samsung hired Dr. Yim-sung Lee, a Stanford Ph.D., who worked for Sharp, GE, and IBM. He in turn brought in Dr. Sang-joon Lee, who was in charge of semiconductor manufacturing process development at Control Data and Honeywell; Dr. Il-bok Lee, who developed 64K DRAMs at Intel and National Semiconductor; Dr. Jong-gil Lee, an expert on improving the production yields at Intersil and Synertek; and Dr. Yong-eui Park, a memory chip designer at Western Digital and Intel.

15   This U.S. subsidiary had a total of 32 researchers, most with doctorates. Samsung Electronics drafted 32 high-potential young engineers from Korea, and partnered them one to one with the U.S.-based researchers,

and instructed them to learn the advanced technologies from their counterparts. These apprentices asked questions and wrote down what they learned in notebooks during the day, as they followed their partners like shadows. At night in their bedrooms the apprentices shared, discussed, and asked about what they had learned during the day. Upon returning to Korea, these men developed 1M DRAM faster than the U.S.-based counterparts (Kang, J. 1996, op. cit. p. 223).

16    Shin, J., and S. Jang. *Dissecting the Secrets of How Samsung Semi-Conductors Became No. 1 in the World* (in Korean). Seoul: Samsung Economic Research Institute, 2006, p. 54.

17    Shin, J., S. Jang, 2006, op cit., p. 50.

## Chapter 3

1    Sony, 1996 Annual Report, p.2.

2    Foroohar, R., and B. Lee. Master of the Digital Age. *Newsweek*, Oct 18, 2004, p. E10.

3    Christensen C. *The Innovator's Dilemma*. Boston: Harvard Business School Press, 1997.

4    Kuzunoki K. Invisible Dimensions of Innovation: Strategy for De-commoditization in the Japanaese Electronics Industry. In C. Herstatt, C. Stockstrom, H. Tschirky, and A. Nagahira, eds. *Management of Technology and Innovation in Japan*. Berlin: Springer, 2006.

5    Henderson, R., and K. Clark. Architectural innovation: The reconfiguration of existing product technologies and the failure of established firms. *Administrative Science Quarterly* 35 (1990), 9–30.

6    Many other researchers have pointed out similar failures of incumbent firms. See Tushman, M., and P. Anderson. Technological discontinuities and organizational environments. *Administrative Science Quarterly* 31 (1986), 439–465; Henderson, R., and K. Clark, Architectural innovation: The reconfiguration of existing product technologies and the failure of established firms. *Administrative Science Quarterly* 35 (1990), 9–30; Anderson, P., and M. Tushman. Technological discontinuities and dominant designs: A cyclical model of technological change. *Administrative Science Quarterly* 35 604–633 (1990); J. Utterback. *Mastering the Dynamics of Innovation*. Boston: Harvard Business School Press, 1994.

7    Ohga, N. *Sony Bombs Hollywood* (in Korean, Original Japanese Title: *Sony No Senritsu*). Seoul: Ruby Box, 2003, p. 281.

8    Kusunoki, ibid.

9    Foroohar, R. and B. Lee. Master of the Digital Age. *Newsweek*, Oct 18, 2004, p. E10.

10    Sony, 1996 Annual Report, p. 2.

11    Sony, 1997 Annual Report, p. 2.

12    Sony, 2002 Annual Report, p. 17.

13    Kunji, I., C. Edwards, J. Greene. Can Sony regain the Magic?; Sure, it still makes great gizmos. But great profits it isn't making. *BusinessWeek*, March 11, 2002.

14    Sony, 2002 Annual Report, p. 11.

15    Id.

16    Samsung Electronics' investment in PDP panels was made through its other group affiliate, Samsung SDI. Samsung Electronics purchased PDPs from Samsung SDI and produced/sold PDP TVs.

17    For instance, Matsushita introduced 40- to 50-inch PDP TVs and sold them very cheaply, capturing over 24% market share. Sharp, on the other hand, actively expanded its LCD market (*Forbes*, Feb 2, 2004).

18    Ramstad, E., and P. Dvorak. Rivals Samsung, Sony Unite in Flat Screen TV Venture. *Wall Street Journal*, July 15, 2004, B1.

19    Dvorak, P., and E. Ramstad. TV Marriage: Behind Sony-Samsung Rivalry, An Unlikely Alliance Develops; Electronics Giants Join Forces On Flat-Panel Technology; Move Prompts Complaints; Uniforms vs. Jackets and Ties. *Wall Street Journal*, January 3, 2006, p. A1.

20    Takuma, M. *Sony Goes Down* (Korean edition, Original Japanese Title: *Gijutsu Kudo*). Seoul: Book Show Company, 2006, p. 162.

21    Sony offered music download services with its own copyright protection software to prevent illegal downloads, OMG (Open Magic Gate) and the ATRAC2 technology, a format previously used for its MiniDisc. This software was very complicated to use, turning consumers away. It was infamous because it allowed customers to copy music files only three times; consumers who frequently formatted their PCs faced the problem of not being able to use music files they had already purchased.

22    Apple took over 70% of the market in the U.S., and 45% in Japan. Even in Japan, Sony's market share was less than 15%. Sony's personal audio business has suffered a sharp drop of sales since 2004, which is attributable to its failure to respond to digital music players in time.

23    Chapter 5 and 6 discuss Sony's problems of global organization. Chapter 7 tells the story of the power struggles inside Sony.

24    Ken Kutaragi. Sony Computer Entertainment. *BusinessWeek*, January 13, 2003, p. 63.

25    Asakura, R. Revolutionaries at Sony. (Korean edition, Original Japanese Title: *Kutaragi Ken No Playstation Kakumei*), Seoul: Golden Owl 2000, p. 30.

26   Mossberg, W. Boss Talk: Shaking Up Sony; Sir Howard Stringer Discusses Formidable Rivals, New Products; Soothing Silence in the Office, *Wall Street Journal*, June 6, 2006, p. B1.

27   Sony, 2002 Annual Report, p. 13.

28   Endo, N. Sony in Chaos (in Japanese), Special Feature, *Weekly Diamond*, February 12, 2005, p. 42.

29   Chapter 6 will discuss how the PlayStation business created many conflicts within Sony, particularly in the development of new digital products.

30   Jin, D. *Manage Passion* (in Korean). Seoul: Kimyoungsa, 2006, p. 294.

31   Chang, S., and J. Podolny. Samsung Electronics' Semiconductor Division. Stanford Business School Case IB24 (A) & (B), 2001.

32   Id.

33   Id.

34   Brull, S., and J. Lim. Samsung's $8 billion Gamble on Upscale Chips. *BusinessWeek*, June 2, 1997, p. 54

35   Id.

36   Wingfield, N. Core Value: At Apple, Secrecy Complicates Life But Maintains Buzz Maker of Mac and iPod Keeps Customers, Workers In Dark. *Wall Street Journal*, June 28, 2006, p. A1; Mossberg, W. The Man; Apple CEO Steve Jobs Talks About The Success of iTunes, Macs's Future, Movie Piracy. *Wall Street Journal*, June 14, 2004, p. B1; Schlender, B. How Big Can Apple Get? *Fortune*, February, 21, 2005, p. 66.; Burrows, P., R. Grover, and T. Lowry, Show Time!: Just As The Mac Revolutionized Computing, Apple Is Changing The World Of Online Music. *BusinessWeek*, February 2, 2004, p. 56; Leonard, D. Songs In The Key Of Steve. *Fortune*, May 12, 2003, p. 52.

37   Shin, Y. 100 million iPods Have Been Sold In Just 5 Years (in Korean). *Chosun Ilbo*, April 11, 2007, p. A20.

## Chapter 4

1    Ohga, N. *Sony Bombs Hollywood* (Korean edition, Original Japanese Title: *Sony No Senritsu*). Seoul: Ruby Box, 2003, p. 10.

2    David, R., and I. Moon, Samsung Design. *BusinessWeek*, December 6, 2004, p. 91.

3    There can be various methodologies for measuring brand value, and each may result in different consequences. For example, the Harris Poll announced that Sony retained the position of number 1 in brand awareness from 2000 to 2006. Sony on Top in Annual Best Brands: Harris

Poll for Seventh Consecutive Year. Harris Interactive Announcement, July 12, 2006. www.harrisinteractive.com.

4    Sony Promotion Division. *Sony Autobiography* (Korean edition. Original Japanese Title: *Sony Jijoden*). Seoul: Sang Sang Books, 1998, p. 137.

5    Morita, A., E. Reingold, and M. Shimomura. *Made in Japan: Akio Morita and Sony*. London: Collins, 1987, p. 79.

6    Ibid., p. 82.

7    Ibid., p. 208.

8    Matsuoka, T. *Sony's Choice, Sony's Success* (Korean edition, Original Japanese Title: *Sony Shinseiki Senryaku*). Seoul: YonhapNews 1999, p. 65.

9    Ibid., p. 65.

10   Ohga, 2003, op. cit., p. 87.

11   This teaser ad format was used in 1989 when Sony released an 8mm camcorder that was the size of a passport, named "CCD TR55."

12   Morita, A., E. Reingold, and M. Shimomura, op. cit., p. 77.

13   Id.

14   The restructuring of PlayStation's distribution system was based on Sony's know-how in the music business, which is characterized by a diversity of items and small production runs. Sony has been accumulating the capability to quickly respond to these demands. This effort was possible only with Kutaragi's innovations in the hardware sector, and a marketing specialist named Sato's applying know-how from music distribution to the game business. In short, this benefit was one of the synergies created by Sony's participation in both the music/film business and the hardware sector. Asakura, R., *Revolutionaries at Sony*. (Korean edition, Original Japanese Title: *Kutaragi Ken No Playstation Kakumei*), Seoul: Golden Owl, 2000.

15   Quelch, J., and A. Harrington. Samsung Electronics: Global Marketing Operations. Harvard Business School Case 9-504051.

16   It is reported that about 2,000 developers in 90 project teams had gone through the VIP program in 2005.

17   Lewis, P. A Perpetual Crisis Machine. *Fortune*, September 19, 2005, p. 58.

18   Id.

19   Moon, I. Camp Samsung. *BusinessWeek*, July 3, 2006, p. 46.

20   Kim, C., and R. Malbaugne. *Blue Ocean Strategy*. Boston: Harvard Business School Press, 2005.

21   Samsung Electronics' VIP team uses a creative problem solving training program called "TRIZ," meaning "Theory of Inventive Problem Solving" in Russian. Lewis, P., op. cit.

22   An employee working at the VIP center says, "This isn't a prison, but we aren't here voluntarily either," Ibid.

23   Kawaso, S., Y. Fujimori, and K. Nihonyanagi. Japan Retail: Consumer Electronics Value Chain. Goldman Sachs, Cross-Sector Report, May 25, 2005.

## Chapter 5

1   May 1988 Speech at the General Management Conference, http://www. sony.net/Fun/SH/1-29/h1.html.

2   Jeon, Y., and J. Han. *Towards a First-class Enterprise: Samsung's Growth and Changes* (in Korean), Seoul: Kimyoungsa, 1994, p.288.

3   Morita, A., E. M. Reingold, and M. Shimomura. *Made in Japan: Akio Morita and Sony.* London: Collins, 1987, p. 155.

4   Ibid., p. 156.

5   See Chapters 8–9 of Nathan, J. *Sony.* New York: Mariner Books, 1999, for more information on the acquisition of Columbia Pictures and its post-acquisition management.

6   Ibid., p. 298.

7   Ibid., p. 301.

8   Ibid., p. 305.

9   Chang, S., C. Yoon, and K. Sohn. Samsung Electronics' Overseas Business Organization 2003. In Chang, S. ed.. *Cases of Korean Companies' Global Management 2,* Seoul: Parkyoungsa, 2004, p. 250.

10   Ibid., p. 250.

11   Ibid., p. 253.

12   Ibid., p. 254.

13   Ibid., p. 254.

## Chapter 6

1   Sony 2001 Annual Report, p. 9

2   Morita, A., E. M. Reingold, and M. Shimomura. *Made in Japan: Akio Morita and Sony.* London: Collins, 1987, pp. 131–132.

3   Sony Promotion Division. *Sony Autobiography* (Korean edition, Original Japanese Title: *Sony Jijoden*). Seoul: SangSangBooks, 1998, p. 391.

4   Iba, T. *From the History of Sony Financial Strategy.* Unpublished manuscript, 2003, p. 36.

5   Sony Promotion Division, op. cit., p. 498.

6    Sony 1998 Annual Report, p. 7

7    See Arthur, W. B. Increasing Returns and the New World of Business. *Harvard Business Review* (1996), 74(4), 100–109; Eisenhardt, K., and D. Sull. Strategy as Simple Rules. *Harvard Business Review* (2001), 79(1), 106–116.

8    Iba, T., op. cit., p. 57.

9    Besides conventional measures such as sales and profit, balance sheet items such as ROE, ROA, and cash flow represented about 30% in 1994, and increased to 35% in 1995.

10   These measures of shareholder value took 80% of all quantitative evaluation and 40% of total evaluation.

11   Miyazaki, T. *The Sinking of Sony* (Korean edition, Original Japanese Title: *Gijutsu Kudo* in Japanese). Seoul: Bookshow Company, 2006, p. 121.

12   Iba, op. cit., p. 62.

13   Miyazaki, op. cit., p. 173.

14   Miyazaki, op. cit., p. 110.

15   Schulhof set up a retailing business, Sony Signature, which sold posters, T-shirts, and souvenirs of Sony Music's singers, and he changed the name of the Loews theater chain, which Sony obtained when it bought Columbia Pictures, to Sony multiplex. He also coaxed Sony Pictures to use sound sources of Sony Music, and vice versa. When making TV ads for a CD player, he wielded his influence to use singers of Sony Music. See Nathan, J. Sony, New York: Mariner Books, 1999, p. 254.

16   Ibid., p. 257.

17   Ibid, p. 260.

18   Kane, Y. and P. Dvorak. Balancing Two Cultures, Sony CEO Tightens Grip. *Wall Street Journal*, March 5, 2007, p. 15.

19   Williamson, O. *Markets and Hierarchies*. New York: Free Press, 1975, ch. 8.

20   Sony 2001 Annual Report, p. 9.

21   Tateishi, Y. *Sony Inside Story* (in Japanese). Tokyo: Kudansha, 2006, ch. 10.

22   NACS was set up to create synergy between hardware and contents, but building an architecture and jump-starting an infrastructure business was a long-term project that required a significant investment. Sony tended to do everything on its own, however, and expected a quick return from this project. Because there was no immediate return, Sony gave up the idea, and members who propelled the business were absorbed into another business unit. It turned out that Sony terminated the project too early because it restarted a business similar to NACS in the Personal Solution Business Group in 2006.

23　Jeon, Y. and J. Han. *Towards a First-class Enterprise: Samsung's Growth and Changes* (in Korean). Seoul: Kimyoungsa, 1994 p. 102.

24　Hankook Economic News. *Why Is Samsung Electronics so Strong* (in Korean). Seoul: Hankook Economic News Press, 2002, p. 38.

25　Jeon, Y. and J. Han. op. cit., p. 73.

26　In December 2007, a special prosecutor was appointed to investigate the bribery of government officials and money laundering charges against Samsung.

27　Ibid., p. 79.

28　PS (profit sharing) is applied to "excess profits," which is defined as the amount exceeding its yearly profit goal: 20% of those excess profits are distributed to employees, who can receive up to 50% of their annual salaries. Several businesses such as semiconductors or mobile communication often receive the maximum PS. For example, in 2006, the target profit level was calculated by applying 14% target profitability to its equity capital of 34.40 trillion won. That year, Samsung Electronics' net income was 7.6 trillion won, 2.8 trillion of which was defined as excess profit. Accordingly, the total PS amount was 560 billion won (2.8 trillion multiplied by 20%), and was distributed to business divisions according to their performance. Employees in the semiconductor and mobile phone businesses received up to a 50% ceiling (*Joong Ang Daily News*, July 11, 2006, p. E3).

29　PI (productivity incentive) is paid based on a semi-annual assessment of business goals and targets. Each department, business unit, and the company as a whole is graded as A, B, or C, based on measures such as EVA, cash flow, and earnings per share etc. for a half year. If the grades for a department, and its business, and the company as a whole are all As, employees in that department will get a bonus of 300% of their annual base payment, but those in the lowest grade will get no bonus. The memory, semiconductors, mobile phone, and TV businesses all got an A for their performance in 2005 and 2006 and got hefty PIs. The nonmemory and home appliance businesses each got a C.

30　During 1997–2006, it was called the "Group Restructuring Office."

31　Cho, I. *There is no Samsung Republic* (in Korean). Seoul: Hankook Economic News Press, 2005, p. 126.

32　Ibid., 2005, p. 245.

33　Holstein, W. Samsung's Golden Touch. *Fortune*, April 1, 2002, p. 89.

34　Cho, H., H. Chun, and S. Lim. *Digital Conqueror Samsung* (in Korean). Seoul: Mail Economic News Press, 2005, p. 31.

## Chapter 7

1   Nathan, J. Sony. New York: Mariner Books, 1999, p. 294.
2   Ramstad, E. Standing Firm: Despite Pressure, Samsung Resists Changing Its Ways; Some Directors, Shareholders Want Better Disclosure As Electronics Giant Grows; Mr. Lee Runs a "Lonely Race." *Wall Street Journal*, March 16, 2005, p. A.1.
3   Tateishi, Y. *Sony Inside Story* (in Japanese). Tokyo: Kudansha, 2006, Ch 2.
4   Nathan, J. op. cit., p. 282.
5   Ibid., p. 249.
6   Ibid., p. 165.
7   Iba, T. *From the History of Sony Financial Strategy*. Unpublished manuscript, 2003, p. 76.
8   Promotion Division. *Sony Autobiography* (in Korean, Original Japanese Title: *Sony Jijoden*) Seoul: SangSangBooks, 1998, p. 7.
9   The new board, organized in June 2003, was comprised of six executive officers including Chairman Idei, President Ando, Corporate Vice Presidents Masaki, Kutaragi, Stringer, and the President of Sony Financial Tokunaga, and ten outside directors, including former ABB Chairman Goran Lindahl, Carlos Ghosn of Nissan, Akishige Okada of Sumitomo Mitsui Bank, Yoshiaki Yamaguchi of Sumitomo Mitsui Financial Group, Yoshihiko Miyauchi of ORIX, Sakie Fukushima of Korn-Ferry International, Yotaro Kobayashi of Fuji Xerox, Hirobumi Kawano of Tokyo Marine and Fire Insurance, and ex-Professor Iwao Nakatani of Hitotsubashi University.
10  Nathan. J. op. cit., p. 297.
11  Another difficult task confronting Idei at that time was negotiating with the Toshiba consortium, pushing for the SD-method, and creating a unified standard for DVD.
12  Tateishi, Y. op. cit., p. 15.
13  Ibid., ch. 11.
14  Ibid., p. 310.
15  Endo, N. Sony's Big Confusion (in Japanese). Special Feature, *The Weekly Diamond*, February 12, 2005.
16  Tateishi, Y. op. cit., p. 286.
17  Ramstad, E., and P. Dvorak. Rivals Samsung, Sony Unite in Flat-Screen-TV Venture. *Wall Street Journal*, July 15, 2004, B.1.
18  He officially retired from Sony in April 2007.
19  Fujiwara, T. *Create Sony* (in Japanese). *Nihon Keizaishinbum*, July 24, 2006, p. 8.
20  Tateishi, Y. op. cit., p. 2006.

21    The stacking method involved stacking the circuits upward, while the trenching method involves digging into the surface of a wafer. Both aim at increasing the density of transistors. At that time, Toshiba took the trench method, and Hitachi the stack. Toshiba suffered setbacks.

22    Lee, K. Kun-hee Lee Essay: Let's Think Before We Look at the World. Seoul: *Donga Ilbo*. 1997, p. 132.

23    Ibid., p. 133.

24    Chang, S., and J. Podolny. Samsung Electronics' Semiconductor Division. Stanford Business School Case IB24 (A) & (B), 2002.

25    Kim, S., and M. Woo. *Kun-hee Lee's Reform 10 Years* (in Korean). Seoul: Kimyoungsa, 2003, p. 171.

26    Lee, K. op. cit., pp. 90-91.

27    Ramstad, E. Standing Firm: Despite Pressure, Samsung Resists Changing Its Ways; Some Directors, Shareholders Want Better Disclosure As Electronics Giant Grows; Mr. Lee Runs a "Lonely Race." *Wall Street Journal*, March 16, 2005, p. A.1.

28    Cho, H., H. Chun, and S. Lim. *Digital Conqueror Samsung Electronics* (in Korean). Seoul: *Maeil Electronic News*, 2005, p. 101.

## Chapter 8

1    Fujiwara, T. *Create Sony* (in Japanese). *Nihon Keizaishinbum*, July 24, 2006, p. 8.

2    Ramstad, E. Standing Firm: Despite Pressure, Samsung Resists Changing Its Ways; Some Directors, Shareholders Want Better Disclosure As Electronics Giant Grows; Mr. Lee Runs a "Lonely Race." *Wall Street Journal*, March 16, 2005, p. A.1.

3    Moon, I. Samsung is Having a Sony Moment: The Korean Titan is Showing Signs of Complacency—and Results Are Suffering. *BusinessWeek*, July 30, 2007, p.38.

4    Sony 2006 Annual Report, p. 7.

5    Sony 2006 Annual Report, p. 5.

6    March, J., and B. Levitt. Organizational Learning. *Annual Review of Sociology* 14 (1988), 319–340.

7    Kane, Y., and P. Dvorak. Balancing Two Cultures, Sony CEO Tightens Grip. *Wall Street Journal*, March 5, 2007, p. 14.

# Glossary

| | |
|---|---|
| ADR | American Depositary Receipt |
| ASIC | Application-Specific Integrated Circuit |
| AV | Audio Video |
| CCD | Charge Coupled Device |
| CDMA | Code Division Multiple Access |
| CD | Compact Disc |
| CRT | Cathode Ray Tube |
| CTO | Chief Technology Officer |
| DDI | Display Driver IC |
| DRAM | Dynamic Random Access Memory |
| DRM | Digital Rights Management |
| DVD | Digital Video Disc |
| ERP | Enterprise Resource Planning |
| GSM | Global System for Mobile communications |
| HAVi | Home Audio Video interoperability |
| HDTV | High Definition TV |
| IEEE | Institute of Electrical and Electronics Engineers |
| IT | Information Technology |
| LCD | Liquid Crystal Display |
| OEM | Original Equipment Manufacturer |
| OLED | Organic Light-Emitting Diode |
| OS | Operating System |

| | |
|---|---|
| PDA | Personal Digital Assistant |
| PDP | Plasma Display Panel |
| SOC | Solution On Chip |
| SRAM | Static Random Access Memory |
| TFT | Thin Film Transistor |
| TFT-LCD | Thin Film Transistor Liquid Crystal Display |
| VAIO | Video Audio Integrated Operation |
| VLSI | Very Large Scale Integration |
| VTR | Video Tape Recorder |

# Index